Economic Challenges Facing Japan's Regional Areas

Tatsuo Hatta
Editor

Economic Challenges Facing Japan's Regional Areas

palgrave
macmillan

Editor
Tatsuo Hatta
Asian Growth Research Institute
Kitakyushu, Fukuoka, Japan

ISBN 978-981-10-7109-6 ISBN 978-981-10-7110-2 (eBook)
https://doi.org/10.1007/978-981-10-7110-2

Library of Congress Control Number: 2017957619

Printed on acid-free paper

This Palgrave Pivot imprint is published by Springer Nature
The registered company is Springer Nature Singapore Pte Ltd.
The registered company address is: 152 Beach Road, #21-01/04 Gateway East, Singapore 189721, Singapore

Foreword

This publication brings together 19 articles originally prepared for an online policy information portal, SPACE NIRA (http://www.spacenira.com/en/), which were released in 2015/2016.

SPACE NIRA was launched by the Nippon Institute for Research Advancement (NIRA) in June 2015 with Dr. Tatsuo Hatta, President of the Asian Growth Research Institute, as its General Editor. NIRA is an independent policy research institute in Tokyo which addresses a wide range of urgent policy issues and formulates focused and timely policy proposals.

For its first year, SPACE NIRA took up issues related to economic challenges for Japan's regional revitalization. Japan's responses to them, and to the problem of an aging population in particular, are of deep interest to the nations outside of Japan. Dr. Hatta selected the topics to be considered in each section and the author of the overview chapter of each section, who then commissioned the experts best suited to address those issues.

Economic Challenges Facing Japan's Regional Areas is a significant and useful reference for all scholars, students, and individuals with an interest in current policy issues in Japan.

Preface

Introduction: Policy Directions to Meet Economic Challenges in Regional Areas

Compared with its metropolitan areas, the productivity of Japan's regional areas is low. Against a per capita production value of 5.54 million yen for the metropolitan areas (represented by Tokyo prefecture and the nation's government-designated cities), the figure for Japan's regional areas is only 3.41 million yen.[1] Regional revitalization therefore represents a much-debated policy issue for Japan.

There are three policy directions in the quest to realize regional revitalization:

(1) subsidy policies (provision of subsidies to targeted cities in regional areas)
(2) regulatory reforms
(3) administrative reforms

Prime Minister Abe's administration (2012 – to the present) has pursued the first and second policies, which are oriented in entirely different directions.

The **subsidy policies** have been carried out within the "Machi, Hito, Shigoto" framework. The intention has been to boost the nation's fertility rate by encouraging young people to move from Tokyo Metropolitan Area (TMA) to the regional areas that receive subsidies as winners of competitions for revitalization proposals.

The Abe administration has also pursued **regulatory reforms**, for example through removing special privileges to Agricultural Cooperatives (JAs) and admitting corporate ownership of agricultural land in a National Strategic Special Zone. It has also allowed *minpaku* (the short-term renting of rooms in private residences or entire residences) for periods as short as two days.

Another approach to promote long-term regional revitalization, but which has not been taken up by the Abe administration, is **administrative reforms** with respect to the allocation of fiscal burdens between municipal governments and the national government. Such reforms would reduce the disincentives for regional municipal governments to provide services to residents.

Of the three types of reforms—subsidy policies, regulatory reforms, and administrative reforms—the latter two may be collectively grouped under the category of "structural reforms."

In reality, subsidy policies seeking to encourage migration of young people from metropolitan areas to regional areas will not lead to long-term regional revitalization. Structural reforms, on the other hand, will be effective in realizing long-term regional revitalization. The purpose of this volume is to demonstrate this fact, and to provide examples of some concrete structural reforms which will be particularly effective in regional revitalization.

Subsidy Policies: Grounded in a Misrecognition of the Facts

I will first demonstrate the ineffectiveness of the Abe administration's subsidy policies.

As part of its "Machi, Hito, Shigoto" fiscal measures, the government spent 1.7 trillion yen in 2015 and 1.8 trillion yen in 2016 on its regional revitalization policy (for promotion of employment in the agricultural sector, for example). By providing subsidies to regional areas, the government seeks to control the influx of population to the TMA in the hope that this will boost the birth rate of the nation as a whole; this is expected to promote national economic growth. However, this policy is based on a serious misunderstanding of the facts. Below, I will demonstrate that the government's "Machi, Hito, Shigoto" fiscal measures are ineffective in stimulating the revitalization of Japan's regions.

The logic of regional revitalization policies is that controlling the concentration of the population in the TMA by strengthening medium-sized cities in regional areas will boost the national fertility rate and increase per capita productivity throughout Japan. However, the premises of this rationale do not accord with reality.

First, it is assumed that population has been flowing into the TMA, giving rise to a unipolar concentration of population in the city. However, from 1965 to 2010, the population growth rate was higher in Sapporo City, Fukuoka City, and Sendai City than in the "major cities in the TMA" (as represented by Tokyo Metropolis plus all the cities with populations of one million or more in the TMA).

Population has been increasing markedly in large cities outside the TMA, as shown in Fig. 1; the overall trend in immigration has been from small cities to large and medium-sized cities throughout the nation. In other words, multipolar concentrations of population have been taking place.

Second, the government considers that encouraging the flow of the younger population away from the TMA, where the fertility rate is lower than it is in Japan's regional areas, is an essential measure to increase the fertility rate.

A comparison of the total fertility rates of cities of over one million people in 2010 (Fig. 2) shows that the rate for Tokyo Metropolis is indeed low among major cities (reaching 1.07 in the area of Tokyo's 23 wards).

However, Fig. 2 shows that Yokohama City, Kawasaki City, Saitama City, Chiba City, and other cities with populations of over one million in the TMA, which function as bed towns for Tokyo Metropolis, all display fertility rates of around 1.30. This figure is higher than that of regional cities such as Sapporo City (1.08), Sendai City (1.21), and Fukuoka City (1.24).

In other words, encouraging migration away from the TMA is contrary to the goal of increasing the fertility rate of the nation.

Third, the government seems to be concerned that population decline will reduce the nation's per capita income. However, data from the past 40 years for Organization for Economic Co-operation and Development (OECD) members indicates that the growth rate of per capita GDP and population growth rate are unrelated. Increasing the rate of growth of the population will not necessarily lead to a growth in productivity (Fig. 3).

Promoting migration away from the TMA therefore does not constitute a growth strategy.

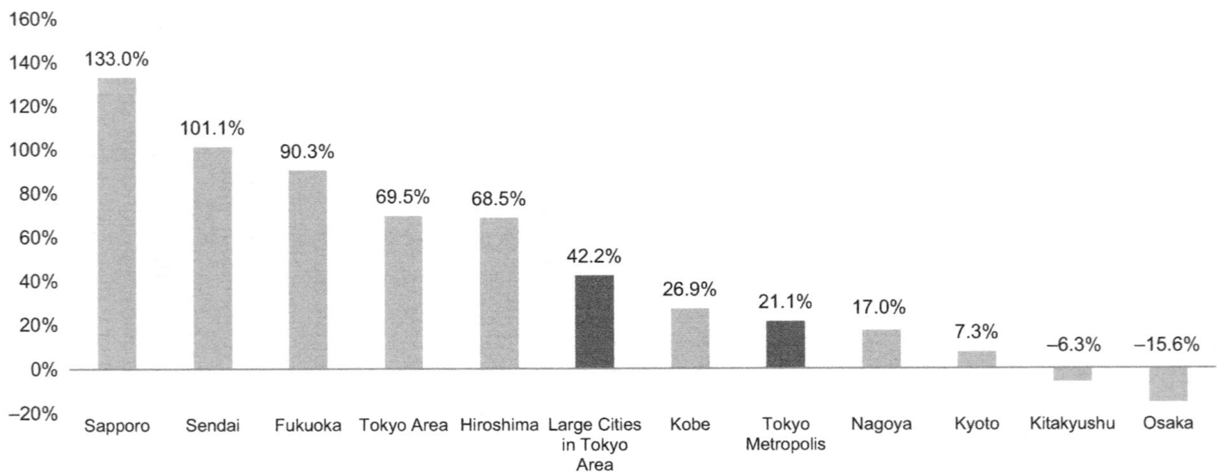

Fig. 1 Rates of population increase in major Japanese cities (1965–2010). Source: Daitoshi Tokei Kyogikai, Daitoshi Tokei Hikaku Nenpyo (Chronological Tables of Comparative Statistical Data for Major Cities). Note 1: Tokyo Area consists of Tokyo Metropolis, Kanagawa Prefecture, Chiba Prefecture, and Saitama Prefecture. Note 2: Large Cities in Tokyo Area consist of Yokohama City, Kawasaki City, Chiba City, Saitama City, and Tokyo Metropolis

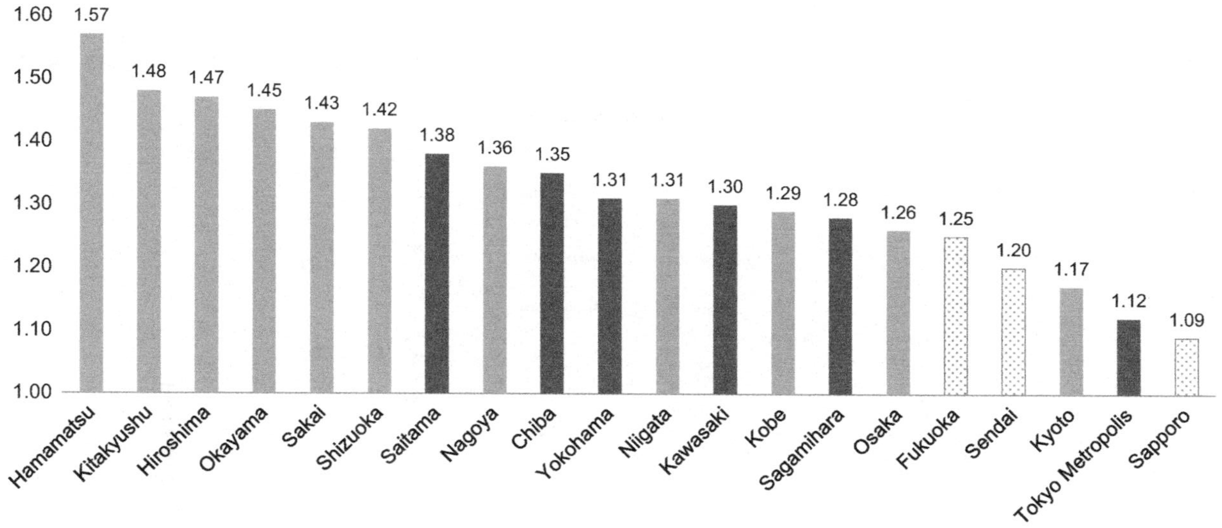

Fig. 2 Total fertility rates of government-designated cities and the Tokyo Metropolitan Area. Source: Vital Statistics 2010, Ministry of Health, Labour and Welfare; Social and Demographic Statistics, Ministry of Internal Affairs and Communications

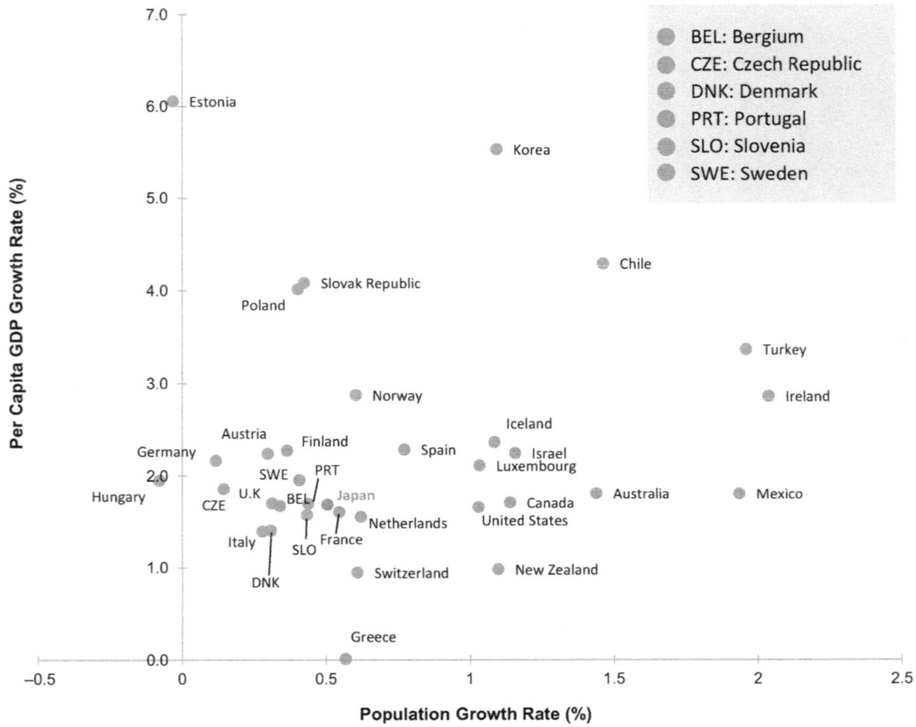

Fig. 3 Growth of per capita GDP and population (average: 1970–2011). Source: OECD Health Statistics 2013; OECD Factbook 2009, 2014

Structural Reforms: Driving Force for Regional Revitalization

Structural reforms remove institutional impediments which limit the growth of the industries in which regional areas possess a comparative advantage. Industries in which regional areas possess a clear comparative advantage are: (1) primary industries such as agriculture and fisheries; (2) the tourist industry; and (3) the elderly services industry. Of these, **barriers to entry** set up to protect existing interests impede the growth of (1) and (2), while the current status of local public finance impedes the growth of (3).

The types of structural reforms effective for regional revitalization can therefore be classified as (1) **regulatory reforms** and (2) **administrative reforms** of local public finance.

The Contents of this Volume

The purpose of this volume is to outline directions for the future expansion of structural reform efforts as economic challenges for regional revitalization.

The present volume is therefore structured as follows:

Group One: Regulatory Reforms

Part I: Agricultural Policy
Part II: Fisheries Policy
Part III: Tourism Policy

Group Two: Administrative Reforms

Part IV: Public Service Sectors for the Elderly
Part V: Measures to Address Japan's Low Birth Rate
Part VI: Local Government Fiscal System

Each part consists of three or four chapters.

A word on Group Two, "Administrative Reforms," is in order. This group begins by discussing regional decentralization measures necessary for the development of the elderly services industry and the childcare industry. It then discusses overall directions for the reform of systems that currently distort incentives for regional municipal governments to provide public goods and services. Part V, "Measures to Address Japan's Low Birth Rate," which analyzes the factors that affect the birth rates of cities, will demonstrate that reform of the regional decentralization system will be more effective than the provision of subsidies to regional municipal governments in promoting regional development in the long run.

In the following we list all the parts of this volume and the authors of the chapters included in each part. The first chapter in each part is an overview chapter.

Group One: Regulatory Reforms

The most effective approach to increase productivity in regional areas is the removal of barriers to entry in industries in which regional areas possess a comparative advantage—the primary industries and the tourism industry.

The Abe administration has taken the first step in reforming JAs (Japan Agricultural Cooperatives) and Agricultural Committees. It must take these reforms further, enabling corporations to own farmland anywhere in the country. Similarly, in the fisheries industry, it will be essential for the government to give corporations the chance to win fishing rights thorough a bidding system rather than continuing to grant monopolies to the Fisheries Cooperative Associations. Deregulation of the practice of *minpaku* will also stimulate the tourism industry in regional areas.

Deregulation that encourages new corporate entries into agriculture and other industries in regional areas would generate a spontaneous upsurge of diverse new ideas, activating regional economies; the government's subsidies for these industries would not. The provision of subsidies to regional areas may, however, be justified in the case of partially compensating for the lost income of those who would lose their existing privileges as a result of structural reforms. This would facilitate the realization of deregulation.

Part I: Agricultural Policy (Masayoshi Honma; Kazunuki Ohizumi and Kazuhito Yamashita)

The key to revitalizing Japan's agricultural industry will be removing the barriers to entry to the industry.

The chapters in Part I emphasize the importance of creating a fully coordinated food supply chain from production to consumption. However, as Kazunuki Ohizumi points out in Chap. 2, the development of a food supply chain of this type has been impeded in Japan by the isolation of the production side from the consumption side by the Staple Foods Act (in the case of rice) and by the system of Designated Producers in the case of milk. Ohizumi argues that the fully fledged promotion of Japan's agricultural industry will necessitate fundamental reform of the systems that separate the two sides.

Kazuhito Yamashita argues in Chap. 3 that it is Japan's JAs that stand behind the antiquated distribution system described by Ohizumi. The functions of the national organization that implemented agricultural regulation on behalf of the national government during the Second World War were carried over into the JA system in the postwar period. This means that the JAs were positioned as the end administrator for the implementation of agricultural policy from their very beginning, and have been granted a variety of special privileges as a result of this status.

Yamashita argues that the JAs have contributed to the decline of Japan's agricultural industry by stubbornly clinging to these special privileges. In particular, the government's policy of maintaining high rice prices has enabled the JAs to continue to collect service fees. The policy of maintaining high rice prices encompasses the reduction of acreage for rice cultivation and the setting of prohibitive tariffs on rice imports. Yamashita argues:

> Despite being protected by high tariffs, Japan's domestic market is shrinking as a result of the decline in the nation's population. The realization of greater price competitiveness for high-quality Japanese rice through the scrapping of the acreage reduction system would not only render tariffs unnecessary, but would also open up export markets throughout the world. This will be the key to the revitalization of Japanese agriculture.

Masayoshi Honma summarizes Part I as follows:

> While the agricultural cooperatives might cling to the old system, farmers are moving forward. Rice farms on a scale of 100 to 200 hectares are appearing throughout the country, and many fruit and vegetable farmers are making use of information and communications technology (ICT) and other new technologies. In the area of dairy farming also, producers and distributors who supply unpasteurized milk without involvement with designated organizations are also appearing.

The issue for agricultural policy will be how to support these new developments, and how to bring the majority of farmers within its purview. It will be important above all not to impede their activities, and essential to fundamentally reform the systems which break up food chains. Further desirable initiatives would be the abolition of the acreage reduction system, the re-examination of the systems governing agricultural land which impede the free acquisition of land, and the adoption of policies to encourage greater efficiency in the operation of agricultural cooperatives and increased competition between the cooperatives in order to further advance the reform of the organizations.

Part II: Fisheries Policy (Masayuki Komatsu; Kojun Hamada and Mari Koyano)

Japan's fishing industry has displayed the most conspicuous decline among OECD member nations. One cause of this decline is the lack of a Total Allowable Catch system for both coastal fishing and deep-sea fishing. Japan employs so-called "Olympic-style" fishing—a system under which all fisheries operators are required to cease fishing when the total catch volume has reached a preset limit. Fisheries operators therefore compete to catch fish as quickly as possible, with the result that juvenile fish are caught. This works against the preservation of fisheries resources.

By contrast, countries including Norway, Canada, and the USA, from which Japan imports fish, apply an Individual Quota (IQ) system, in which a specific catch volume is allocated to each ship. Because of this, all ships attempt to catch only mature fish of the size with the highest market value. This has the effect of preserving resources. The application of this system in Japan has been prevented by opposition from existing fisheries operators.

However, Japan's first IQ system has been recently applied to shrimp fishing on Sado Island. Kojun Hamada's chapter discusses the effects of the introduction of this system. Under this project, fishermen have been able to harvest shrimp during the period when unit prices are highest. This has increased average prices and offered the shrimp fishermen significant benefits in a short period. Mari Koyano's chapter provides an overview of the current status of management of sea urchin and sea cucumber resources, and presents an evaluation of the legal issues surrounding the management of these resources.

In Chap. 4, Masayuki Komatsu indicates that the introduction of this first IQ system was made possible by the participation of the Niigata Prefecture administration.

Part III: Tourism Policy (Yasushi Shinohara; Yoshitaka Mizoo and Kumiko Tomikawa)

The tourism industry is one in which each regional area possesses an individual comparative advantage. The number of inbound tourists to Japan is growing rapidly, and exceeded 20 million in 2016. As Yasushi Shinohara indicates in Chap. 7, the easing of existing tourism-related regulations affecting the acceptance of foreign tourists will raise the quality of tourism services in the nation.

The most essential regulatory reform related to the tourism industry in Japan is reform in the area of *minpaku*. With the increasing number of inbound tourists, the shortage of floor space in Japan's hotels has become more apparent. Moreover, tourists from overseas want to experience the Japanese lifestyle, and would therefore often prefer to stay in private homes rather than hotels. Normal houses are also more convenient, offering access, for example, to kitchens and washing machines.

In recent years, the development of easily accessible accommodation-intermediary services such as Airbnb has resulted in the increasing offering of *minpaku* accommodation in Japan. But this is, strictly speaking, illegal, because it has been stipulated that an individual or business renting out a residence for a period of less than one month is regarded as a hotel business, and must satisfy all the requirements of a hotel business, such as having a front desk.

In response to these new developments, *minpaku* was legalized for a stay longer than six days within National Strategic Special Zones, and the first reform measures have been put into effect in Tokyo's Ota Ward. In addition, in September 2016 it became possible to offer *minpaku* accommodation for periods from two days and upwards in National Strategic Special Zones throughout the nation.

The Act on Land and Building Leases does not stipulate a minimum rental period, and rooms therefore technically can be rented for periods commencing from one night. However, Article 2 of the Hotel Business Act defines a hotel business as one that provides accommodation in exchange for a fee, and specifies the conditions defining accommodation as the use of bedding. In other words, in practice, a rental arrangement which involves the provision of a change of sheets is regarded as a hotel business. Therefore, *minpaku* arrangements, which involve renters fixing their own meals and doing their own washing, represent a rental of a normal residence. The considerable political power of the hotel industry has, as it were, produced a distortion of the law, resulting in the application of restrictions.

Returning to a more natural interpretation of rental business and hotel business, the ***minpaku*** allowed in National Strategic Special Zones is defined as house rentals, and offered under conditions such as the keeping of a register of renters by the landlord (in part as an anti-terrorism measure) and the establishment of a liaison to resolve any trouble that may arise with neighbors. The background to this development is discussed by Kumiko Tomikawa in Chap. 9.

An important requirement for the revitalization of the tourism industry in regional areas will be that each region takes the lead with regard to tourism services in its own region, as pointed out by Yoshitaka Mizoo in Chap. 8. The formulation of tourism plans for specific regions suited to a diverse range of tourists will be indispensable to the development of tourist areas. Traditionally, however, only specialized travel managers who had passed an examination covering a wide range of subjects were authorized to formulate travel plans. Thus, individuals possessing expertise related only to a specific region could not pass the required examination, and therefore have not been put to use in responding to the increase in inbound tourism. Because of this, a new qualification enabling travel managers to formulate travel plans for a specific region has been established in Semboku City, a National Strategic Special Zone. If this relaxation of restrictions were to be extended to the entire country, it would be possible to realize the region-led revitalization of the tourism industry proposed by Mizoo throughout Japan.

Group Two: Administrative Reforms

Another type of reform that will be effective in promoting regional revitalization is **administrative reform** of the system of allocation of fiscal burdens between municipal governments and the national government. However, this is not a simple matter of pushing ahead with regional decentralization.

The types of services that municipal governments offer may be classified as the following:

(1) Provision of standardized national services for residents, such as medical care, education, and social security. The national government requires local governments to offer such services at or above a standard level throughout the nation.
(2) Provision of local public goods, such as community centers, libraries, and concert halls. Each municipal government is expected to choose its level of service provision.

The national government is responsible for all expenses for the former services, while municipal governments are responsible for the expenses of the latter services.

However, a certain level of fiscal adjustment by the national government is considered necessary in order to reduce the disparities in ability-to-pay between different municipalities. This may be called "fiscal equalization."

The resulting division of fiscal responsibility between the national government and municipal governments is shown by ① through ③ in Table 1. The principle here is that the national government decides the amount of fiscal resources to be allocated for the services it provides, and municipal governments have complete discretion in the application of fiscal resources for the services they provide.

In actuality, however, the current system for the division of the fiscal burden functions not as shown by ① through ③, but as shown by ④ through ⑦. In other words, municipal governments are granted discretion in disbursing fiscal resources which they should not disburse at their discretion, as shown in ⑤, while they are granted only a small margin of discretion in relation to resources over which they should have complete discretion, as shown in ⑥. This situation distorts incentives for municipalities to provide services.

Box ① in Table 1 encompasses services which should be solely financed by the national government, but in reality municipalities are required to partially finance them, as shown in ⑤. This gives municipalities an incentive to control any influx of elderly residents into the municipality, because this will reduce its financial burden. This is discussed in Parts IV and V.

Local public goods need to be financed in part by municipal governments and in part by the national government, as fiscal equalization measures between municipalities. Part VI, which considers the system of local public finances, demonstrates that incentives for municipal governments are distorted even with respect to the provision of public goods.

Table 1 Discretion of municipal governments over expenditure

Category of expenditure		(a) National-level services (Medical services, education, protection of livelihood, etc.)		(b) Local public goods (Community centers, concert halls, elderly services, etc.)	
Resources	In principle	① Central government		② Municipal government	③ Central government (Fiscal equalization)
	In reality	④ Central government	⑤ Municipal government	⑥ Municipal government	⑦ Central government (Fiscal equalization)

Revenue the amount of which municipal governments cannot control

Revenue the amount of which municipal governments should control in principle, but cannot in reality

Revenue the amount of which municipal governments can control

Part IV: Public Service Sectors for the Elderly (Wataru Suzuki; Yasushi Iwamoto and Masayoshi Hayashi)
Regional areas, in which land rents are lower, clearly possess a comparative advantage in the provision of elderly services, such as the establishment and management of nursing homes.

Nevertheless, few retirees move to regional areas. One reason for this is that regional municipalities do not welcome influxes of elderly residents. For example, municipal governments are often reluctant to allow the construction of new care facilities in their nursing care project plans. Migration of the elderly from metropolitan areas to regional areas disadvantages regional municipal governments, because these governments are then required to shoulder a considerable financial burden for social insurance (nursing care insurance, National Health Insurance, etc.), while the elderly pay only a small amount in local taxes.

In the case of National Health Insurance, the central and prefectural governments only finance a part of the medical benefits. The remainder is financed by insurance premiums and by the tax revenue of the municipal government. This means that the financial burden on the municipality increases as the number of elderly residents increases. The same is true of nursing care insurance. As Masayoshi Hayashi points out, this provides municipal governments with an incentive to discourage the immigration of elderly citizens into their regions by not approving the construction of new care facilities.

In Chap. 10, Wataru Suzuki summarizes the view that municipal governments would welcome an influx of elderly residents if the public financing system were reformed to ensure that such an influx would not increase the social-insurance related financial burden on the municipal governments.

In the case of National Health Insurance, these reforms would involve:

(1) maintenance of the current municipality-based framework;
(2) calculation of a "model benefit" for people in each age cohort based on the average per person benefits for that age cohort throughout the entire country (the older the cohort, the higher the model benefit amount would be, reflecting the higher risk of illness);
(3) provision by the national government of an amount corresponding to the model benefit to each participant (this represents the "risk structure adjustment" between municipalities proposed by Yasushi Iwamoto in Chap. 11);

(4) provision by municipalities of the excess of the total realized benefit payments over the total model benefit payments for local elderly insurance subscribers.

As a result, National Health Insurance for the elderly would be financed in principle by national tax revenue alone rather than by regional taxes or insurance premiums. This mechanism would reduce the average burden on municipalities to zero. However, if, for example, a municipality were negligent in applying preventive measures, resulting in the payment of benefits higher than the model benefit for a resident's age, then the difference would be made up by the municipality.

If these reforms were implemented, influxes of elderly people would be welcomed by regional municipalities since they would bring with them the model benefits financed by the central government. Municipal governments would then begin to approve the construction of new care facilities more willingly than before. The regional cities which succeeded in attracting retirees would also benefit from increased sustainable employment opportunities in the services industry. As a result, young people would also move to the regional cities. As this demonstrates, regional areas can achieve growth through their specific comparative advantages.

In Chap. 12, Masayoshi Hayashi reveals that the same problems are also found in the nursing care insurance system. He unravels the complex division of the financing burden of the existing National Health Insurance system among various levels of government.

In Chap. 13, Hatta (2017) elucidates the proposal and estimates that the "the model benefit" or "standardized expense" for the national health insurance would be 125,000 yen for each additional resident younger than 65, and 556,000 yen for each additional resident older than 65.

Part V: Measures to Address Japan's Low Birth Rate (Tatsuo Hatta; Masayuki Nakagawa and Wataru Suzuki)

In order to address the nation's declining fertility rate, the government believes it is necessary to encourage migration of the younger population away from the TMA, because the fertility rate of Tokyo is among the lowest of large cities in Japan. However, as Fig. 2 shows, Yokohama City, Kawasaki City, Saitama City, Chiba City, and other cities with populations of over one million which function as bed towns for the Greater Tokyo Area all display fertility rates of around 1.30. This figure is higher than that of regional cities such as Sapporo City (1.08), Sendai City (1.21), and Fukuoka City (1.24). This indicates that encouraging migration away from the TMA is inconsistent with the original goal of increasing the fertility rate of the nation as a whole.

Why, then, is the fertility rate of Tokyo itself low? In Chap. 15, Masayuki Nakagawa argues as follows: Female students and new graduates move to Tokyo from regional areas for education or in search of employment. When these women marry and look towards starting a family, they move to suburban cities such as Chiba and Saitama to take advantage of lower rents. Because of this, the fertility rate of Tokyo remains low, while the fertility rates of its peripheral cities are relatively high.

In the case of the majority of other large cities in Japan, a significant proportion of the suburban areas are incorporated within the boundaries of the city area itself, and their fertility rates are therefore higher than that of Tokyo, where the greater proportion of the suburban areas are outside the city area. According to Nakagawa, the data indicate that in the cases of Sendai City, Fukuoka City, and Sapporo City, the marriage rate is high in the suburbs and low in the central city. That is, the trend observed in Tokyo is also observed in these cities. Therefore, the fiscal measures being pursued by the government to encourage young people to move to regional areas from the TMA will be ineffective as a measure to increase the fertility rate of the nation as a whole.

Instead, reform of the local public finance system would be effective for this purpose. Wataru Suzuki argues that the system of local public finances has needlessly lengthened the waiting list for childcare in various areas of the TMA, and has reduced the fertility rates of these areas.

According to Suzuki, municipalities which expand their budgets for childcare will find themselves facing an influx of "childcare refugees" from surrounding municipalities, which will have the effect of increasing the city's expenditure on childcare. This explains why large cities with long childcare waiting lists find it difficult to shorten these lists even if they initially expand their childcare budgets.

The fundamental solution to this problem is for the central government to provide a model benefit for childrearing support measures to each of the nation's municipalities. With this model benefit, the central government would finance municipalities for the full amount necessary for standard childcare services. As a result, municipalities would experience zero burden in implementing standard childrearing support measures. Thus, the increase in childcare expenses due to population influx would be matched by increased support from the government, thus eliminating the problem of undersupply of childcare services. This reform of fiscal measures would allow municipalities to develop childcare facilities as desired, with no concern over an influx of "childcare refugees." All things considered, this could be expected to have a significant effect in addressing Japan's declining birth rate.

Note that the concept of the central government's provision of "model benefits" for childcare support discussed in Part V is closely related to that for health and nursing cares for the elderly discussed in Part IV.

Part VI: Local Government Fiscal System (Motohiro Sato; Wataru Kobayashi and Tomomi Miyazaki)

Turning now to the allocation of the fiscal burden for local public goods, a portion is funded by municipalities themselves (② in Table 1), and a portion is financed by the national government (③ in Table 1) as a fiscal equalization measure.

In Chap. 19, Tomomi Miyazaki indicates that in the case of ②, which municipalities themselves should be able to finance at their own discretion, it is actually institutionally difficult for municipalities to exercise their discretion, as indicated in ⑥. This difficulty is caused, among other things, by the fact that the effective property tax rate is reduced for small residences as a special measure (reducing the value evaluation standard for taxation to one-sixth of the assessed value). The property tax is thus not functioning as a benefit tax. Miyazaki recommends reforms to ensure full levying of property tax as a benefit tax.

On the other hand, the portion of the expenditure financed by fiscal equalization measures from the central government, over which, in principle, municipalities should not exercise their own discretion (③ in Table 1), can actually be increased by the municipalities, shifting the resulting fiscal burden to the central government.

Moreover, because the government guarantee of fiscal resource provision extends to local government bonds, the interest rate of these bonds has been reduced to the level of government bonds. As Motohiro Sato points out in Chap. 17, this "low rate of interest on local government bonds renders the actual cost of public projects and public facilities (including risk) unclear."

Sato goes on to indicate that local residents are hardly aware of the costs involved in policies and projects decided on by local governments. He attributes this to the fact that "local governments have previously functioned as little more than subsidiary organs of the central government, implementing policies and projects that the central government formulated and financed."

In order to address this issue, in Chap. 18 Wataru Kobayashi points to three important issues related to local allocation tax grants: (1) the scope of and standards for the guaranteed fiscal resources; (2) the measurement of the "ability-to-pay" of local governments; and (3) reform of the fiscal system for local governments not receiving local allocation tax grants.

Conclusion: The Structural Reforms Essential to Regional Revitalization

The key to an economic growth strategy is to transfer resources from low-productivity sectors to high-productivity sectors.

Companies involved in primary industry and the elderly services industry can achieve a high level of productivity in regional areas, with their rich natural environments and broad areas of land. By contrast, most companies involved in cutting-edge international industries can achieve high productivity in large cities, where they can take advantage of the agglomeration economy.

Regional revitalization initiatives based on the "Machi, Hito, Shigoto" framework are attempting to encourage the relocation of corporations engaged in cutting-edge industries in metropolitan areas to regional areas, while leaving in place the existing systems that impede corporate participation in primary industry or the migration of the elderly to regional areas. Such policies are similar to refusing access to the sports field to a child with an outstanding talent for baseball and offering that child nothing but mathematics textbooks.

If companies, young people, and the elderly are able to freely migrate between regional areas and metropolitan areas, they will be able to choose the location in which they will achieve their highest productivity. This approach to regional revitalization fits in with the "third arrow" of Abenomics. Reform of regulations to allow the entry of companies to the agricultural, tourist, and childcare and elderly services industries in regional areas, in addition to the reform of local public finance, will be essential to the realization of the potential of Japan's regional areas.

Asian Growth Research Institute, Kitakyushu, Japan Tatsuo Hatta

Note

1. Calculated from 2013 prefectural accounts (production-side; actual) and estimated population. Note that Shizuoka City, Sakai City, Hamamatsu City, Sagamihara City, and Kumamoto City do not announce total production figures, and are therefore not included among government-designated cities here.

Contents

List of Figures

List of Maps

List of Tables

PART I

Regulatory Reforms: Agricultural Policy

CHAPTER 1

Agricultural Policy: Supporting the New Developments in Japan's Agriculture

Masayoshi Honma

Abstract Japan's agriculture is changing both in the field and in policy terms. The first change is the development of new farm activities and a system of distribution of agricultural products, and the other is the breaking up of the "iron triangle" which has been the foundation of Japan's agricultural policy to date.

In the field, managers practicing advanced agricultural management are beginning to appear. But the creation of food value chains based on "market in" strategies is lagging behind, and is being impeded by Japan's distribution system.

Japan's Agricultural Cooperatives (JAs) are the institutions behind the distribution problems. The Abe administration is working to break up the "iron triangle" which includes JAs, but the process is still underway. Further reform is desirable.

Keywords Agricultural policy • Food chain • Market in • Liberal Democratic Party • Ministry of Agriculture • Forestry and Fisheries • Agricultural Cooperatives • "iron triangle" • Agricultural Cooperative reform • Abe administration • Council for Regulatory Reform

M. Honma (✉)
Department of Economics, Seinan Gakuin University, Fukuoka, Japan

T. Hatta (ed.), *Economic Challenges Facing Japan's Regional Areas*,
https://doi.org/10.1007/978-981-10-7110-2_1

Change is coming to Japan's agriculture. Irrespective of the fate of the Trans-Pacific Partnership (TPP) negotiations, the nation's agricultural sector must formulate a new survival strategy and create twenty-first-century business models. More than a movement away from Japan's long-lasting postwar agricultural policy, this represents an escape from the "1940 system," created during the Second World War, in the sense that it has formed the basis of that postwar agricultural policy (Honma 2014).

What we are witnessing is the collapse of the "iron triangle" formed by the Liberal Democratic Party (LDP), the Ministry of Agriculture, Forestry and Fisheries, and the agricultural cooperatives. With the re-examination of the acreage reduction policy and the reform of the agricultural cooperative system, agricultural policy is beginning to move in a very different direction from its previous course (Honma 2015). New fruit and vegetable businesses, which have not been reliant on policy measures for their establishment, are also being nurtured (The 21st Century Public Policy Institute 2016). The points for discussion offered here will consider Japan's agriculture from two perspectives.

The first perspective is that of the development of a new agriculture. Throughout Japan, entirely new agricultural businesses are being created, and the possibilities for Japanese agriculture are multiplying. However, problems can also be observed. Can agricultural policy contribute to their solution?

At the same time, Japan's traditional agriculture is in a state of deadlock, and is undergoing a process of decline. What is causing this? Our second point for discussion concerns the re-examination of the system which has traditionally underpinned Japan's agricultural policy, and the escape from that system. Rather than the LDP or the Ministry of Agriculture, Forestry and Fisheries, it is the agricultural cooperatives which are clinging to the old system. Why is this?

In Chap. 2, Kazunuki Ohizumi addresses our first point for discussion. First, Dr. Ohizumi considers the initiatives implemented by practitioners of advanced farm management, and finds that the points they have in common are the adoption of market-oriented strategies which emphasize product development based on consumer needs, and a focus on the creation of food chains which encompass the entire flow from producer to consumer. However, these food chains are not yet sufficiently strong, and despite efforts to increase added value, such initiatives do not transcend the domain of the "individual value chain" and have little influence on the surrounding agricultural milieu (Ohizumi 2018).

Dr. Ohizumi indicates that it is the system of distribution based on product-oriented approaches which impedes the creation of food chains. The Staple Food Act in the case of rice, the Wholesale Market Act in the case of vegetables, meat and flowers, and the system of designated organizations for the production of raw milk—all these systems related to agricultural products serve to separate the domains of production and consumption. The separation of producers from consumers fosters the delusion that producers exist independently. This nurtures a culture which rejects cooperation with other industries and the entry of outsiders to the sector, impeding the creation of food chains. In order to realize a fully fledged new direction for Japanese agriculture, it will be essential to fundamentally reform the system which separates producer and consumer.

Taking up our second point for discussion, in Chap. 3 Kazuhito Yamashita argues that Japan's agricultural cooperatives are the driving force behind the system described by Dr. Ohizumi. The national system responsible for the administration of agricultural production during the Second World War was carried over into the agricultural cooperative system in the postwar period. Japan's agricultural cooperatives are therefore not independent bodies, but rather government-administered organizations. They were positioned from their inception as the organs responsible for the ultimate implementation of agricultural policy, and have been granted a variety of special privileges as a result (Yamashita 2018).

Dr. Yamashita argues that in seeking to maintain their privileges, the agricultural cooperatives have in fact contributed to the decline of Japanese agriculture. In particular, they have adhered to a policy of high rice prices in order to maintain commissions, and have thus continued a policy of reducing the acreage under cultivation on rice farms for more than 45 years. In order to enable this, they have set prohibitively high rice tariffs to discourage imports, and have opposed the reduction of tariffs by the World Trade Organization (WTO) or through the establishment of the TPP.

The efforts of the Abe Cabinet toward reform of the agricultural cooperatives have produced certain outcomes, but are still in progress. In the area of rice policy, a transition toward the production of fodder rice is proceeding as a new form of the acreage reduction system. Dr. Yamashita suggests that the scrapping of this policy, which entails enormous subsidies, and the transition to a system of direct payments to protect farmers while allowing the market to determine the price of rice would reduce the disparity between domestic and overseas rice prices, increasing the potential for export (Yamashita 2015).

Political reform will also be necessary to enable Japan to exit the old system, and the dissolution of the "iron triangle" would be one desirable initiative. The conditions are auspicious. The former Minister for Agriculture, Forestry and Fisheries has a background in trading companies rather than agricultural interests and the current Minister is a former official of the Ministry of Economy, Trade and Industry. The minister responsible for overseeing the Council for Regulatory Reform, which is the driving force behind reform of the agricultural cooperatives, is passionate regarding agricultural reform, and this is another factor which has been behind the Cabinet-led push for reform of the agricultural cooperatives. We can regard the era when political supporters of the agricultural sector came together with an immovable resolution to defeat reform proposals as over.

These changes in the political climate are being observed because agriculture itself is changing. While the agricultural cooperatives might cling to the old system, farmers are moving forward. Rice farms of 100–200 hectares are appearing throughout the country, and many fruit and vegetable farmers are making use of information and communications technology (ICT) and other new technologies. In the area of dairy farming also, producers and distributors who supply raw milk without involvement with designated organizations are also appearing.

The issue for agricultural policy will be how to support these new developments, and how to bring the majority of farmers within its purview. It will be important above all not to impede their activities, and essential to fundamentally reform the systems which break up food chains. Further desirable initiatives would be the abolition of the acreage reduction system, the re-examination of the systems governing agricultural land which impede the free acquisition of land, and the adoption of policies to encourage greater efficiency in the operation of agricultural cooperatives and increased competition between the cooperatives in order to further advance the reform of the organizations.

References

Honma, Masayoshi (2014), *Nogyo Mondai: TPP Go Nosei wa Koukawaru* (Agricultural Problems: How the TPP will Change Agricultural Policy), Chikumashobo Ltd (in Japanese).

Honma, Masayoshi (2015), "The TPP and agricultural reform in Japan," in A. George Mulgan and M. Honma (eds.), *The Political Economy of Japanese Trade Policy*, Palgrave Macmillan, pp. 94–122.

Ohizumi, Kazunuki (2018), "A New Direction for Agriculture in Japan," in T. Hatta (ed.), *Economic Challenges Facing Japan's Regional Areas*, Plagrave Macmillan, pp. 9–17.

The 21st Century Public Policy Institute (2016), *Atarashii Nogyo Bijinesu wo Motomete* (Pursuit of New Agricultural Businesses), Research Project Report, February 2016 (in Japanese).

Yamashita, Kazuhito (2015), *Nihon Nogyo wa Sekai ni Kateru* (Japanese Agriculture Can Compete with the World), Nikkei Publishing Inc (in Japanese).

Yamashita, Kazuhito (2018), "Japan's Agricultural Policy: Escaping the *Ancien Régime*," in T. Hatta (ed.), *Economic Challenges Facing Japan's Regional Areas*, Plagrave Macmillan, pp. 19–27.

CHAPTER 2

A New Direction for Agriculture in Japan

Kazunuki Ohizumi

Abstract The only means available to Japan to increase the total production value of the nation's agriculture is the expansion of the sector of farm management which generates the highest production value, in particular "advanced agricultural management," which generates sales of over 50 million yen per year.

The business foundation for management of this type is provided by the creation of food chains with the "market in" concept. A food chain can be considered as a single linked system incorporating all functions related to food supply, from the production of agricultural goods to their processing, distribution, and consumption. This type of agriculture is termed "food chain agriculture" in this chapter. This chapter offers a discussion of the characteristics of food chain agriculture and the potential of Japanese agriculture.

Keywords Food chain agriculture • Advanced agricultural management • Market in • Value chain • "sextiary industry" • Agriculture–commerce–industry collaboration • Contract cultivation • Horizontal division of labor • Vertical integration

K. Ohizumi (✉)
The 21st Century Public Policy Institute, Tokyo, Japan

T. Hatta (ed.), *Economic Challenges Facing Japan's Regional Areas*,
https://doi.org/10.1007/978-981-10-7110-2_2

1 Introduction

I believe that in order to increase Japan's agricultural output, we ultimately have no choice but to rely upon the small proportion of the nation's farms which produce a high output. My expectations in this respect are particularly high for farms under advanced farm management, management which produces sales volumes of 50 million yen or more per year. While constituting less than 1% of Japan's farms, these enterprises produce one-third of the nation's agricultural output.

Agricultural business strategies of this type are known by a variety of names—contract farming (planned production), agriculture–commerce–industry cooperation, integration, the "sextiary sector," and so forth—but their common basis is agriculture positioned within a food chain flowing from downstream to upstream, with agricultural production based on market needs.[1]

A food chain can be considered as a linked chain of functions related to the supply of food, stretching from the growing or raising of agricultural products, through processing and distribution, to consumption. None of these functions exists independently of the others; they are mutually related within a single flow up to the ultimate consumption (or sale) of the product, and each operates in cooperation with the others.

When a food chain is created, mutual links between processes are close, and information is able to flow in both directions between upstream and downstream. Because of this, factors including the quality, form, and price of the product and the distribution routes demanded by the market can be known prior to production, and production can be planned accordingly. Production of this type is necessarily production based on the needs of the consumer, or in other words, "market-oriented" production.

A number of cases will be taken up below in order to consider the level of diffusion of these business strategies.

2 Developing a New Agriculture through the Creation of Food Chains

Food chains are being created by a variety of processes seeking to add value to agricultural products; in Japan, these processes are termed the "sextiary sector," agriculture–industry–commerce cooperation, and "integration." The "sextiary sector" is being brought into existence where agricultural policy is actively striving to create food value chains. Here, agricultural producers are increasing their profitability by expanding from the simple sale of agricultural products into high value-added businesses such as food processing and the service industry. By contrast, the frameworks termed agriculture–industry–commerce cooperation and integration involve companies taking the initiative to create more rationalized food chains. Production based on the needs of processing and marketing companies results in the realization of high value-added agricultural products. This category includes Calbee, Nippon Ham, Ise Farm, and Frieden. While the "sextiary sector" and integration differ in that farmers and companies are their respective driving forces, they each involve the creation of food chains based on vertical divisions of labor. Agriculture–industry–commerce cooperation, by contrast, involves the creation of food chains based on a horizontal division of labor between farmers and companies.

Planned production based on contracts, marketing activities, and the acceptance of orders is also increasing in areas involving the production of fresh produce rather than processed foodstuffs, specifically the rice and vegetable agriculture industries. In the case of rice agriculture, a model in which rice distributors take the needs of the food services industry and similar sales channels into consideration and play a coordinating role with rice producers has recently become increasingly common in Japan. Large-scale farms including Uchida Farm (Kumamoto Prefecture; 50 hectares), Tanaka Farm (Tottori Prefecture; 100ha), Yokota Farm (Ibaraki Prefecture; 100ha), Sometani Farm (Chiba Prefecture; 108ha), and Fukuhara Farm (Shiga Prefecture; 160ha) are among the businesses which have adopted this model and increased their size (Map 2.1).

In the area of vegetable agriculture, a pattern in which farmers conduct direct marketing activities to retailers and restaurants, leading to the receipt of orders and the introduction of planned production, can be widely observed. Wagoen in Chiba Prefecture, Top River in Nagano Prefecture, Misuzu Life in Nagano Prefecture, and Yasai Club in Gunma Prefecture are among these.

In cases in which the food services industry and logistics companies involve themselves in the production of fresh produce, we are seeing a model of planned production based on the particular needs of specific companies and the volumes of produce they require. Valor in Gifu Prefecture, Seven Farm in Chiba and other prefectures, Watami Farm in Hokkaido and other prefectures, and AEON AGRI CREATE in Saitama

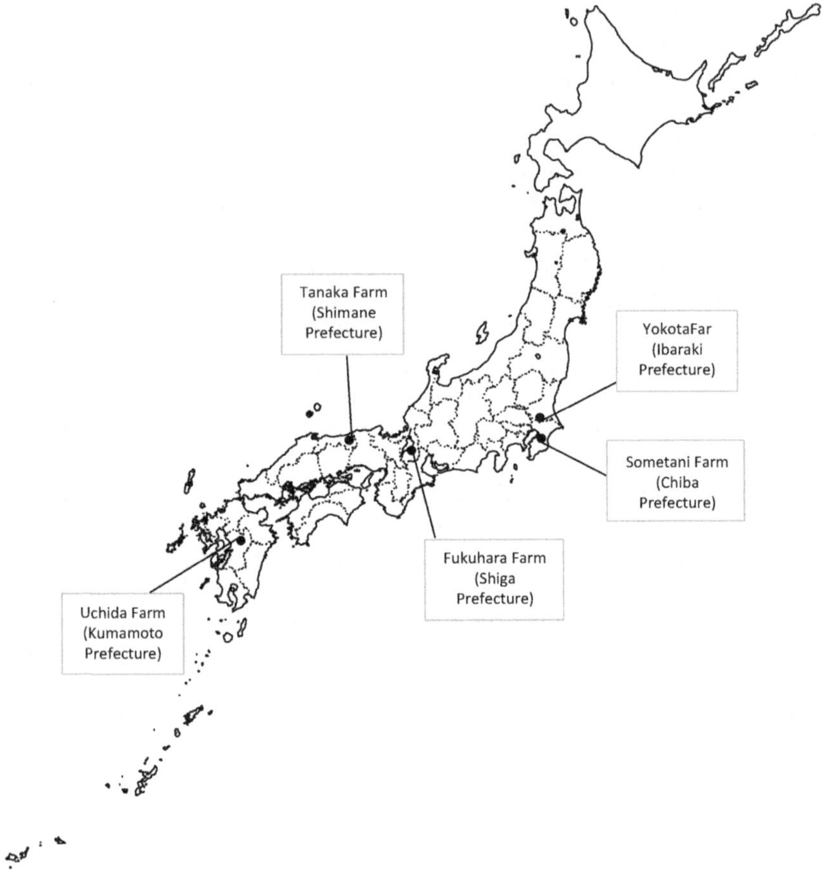

Map 2.1 Large-scale farms in Japan. Note: This map was prepared by the author.

Prefecture are among the businesses employing this model. As we have seen, corporate involvement in agriculture is leading to the creation of food chains based on a vertical division of labor; in other cases, food chains are being created involving a horizontal division of labor.

In each case, elements including the quantity to be shipped, the period for delivery, and price are decided prior to production, and production is planned in order to enable the targets to be met. Whether the development of a food chain is an explicit goal or not, food chains are created between the participants in market-oriented planned production.

It has been indicated that cases in which corporate involvement in agriculture and the development of a "sextiary sector" have failed have been due to an inability to create sales channels as projected. These failures have been due to the adoption of a "product-oriented" approach. A product-oriented approach prioritizes the inclinations and circumstances of the agricultural producer in deciding on specific products and production volumes. It might be said that for such an approach, the entire process is over when the product appears. In the case of agriculture, however, the adoption of a "market-oriented" approach, the creation of sales channels, and the creation of a food chain are at the apex of Key Factors for Success (KFS).

3 Realizing Growth in Agriculture by Means of Advanced Farm Management

The shared point in all of these initiatives is that they are market-oriented businesses involved in food chains. But the adoption of a market-oriented approach is not as simple a matter as it may appear. Agriculture is an industry which innately involves high levels of uncertainty, due to factors including environmental conditions and insect damage. Even when production plans are formulated based on the needs of the market, production often fails to proceed according to plan. This necessitates a large number of corrections and solutions. Advanced farm management implements these solutions proactively in order to increase output. This increases the scale of farms and boosts productivity, realizes high value-added agricultural products, and increases employment and ties between farm managers in farming communities.

With regard to the achievement of increased productivity, the reorganization of all agricultural production procedures based on contracts, for example rice farmers extending their cropping period by deciding on the specific fields to plant and the date to plant by calculating backwards from the date of shipping, reduces machinery depreciation costs and enables the economic allocation of labor resources, resulting in significant cost reductions. This enables farm management to look towards 100ha operations, as indicated above. This is because when prices and the volume of production are decided prior to production, it is possible to introduce measures to increase profits in accordance with the specific arrangement. Such efforts to increase productivity are not restricted to rice farming.

Advanced farm management collects and makes use of all the data involved, making it possible to conduct focused management (for example, by deciding on the critical amount of stock feed to be produced or allocating the use of machinery on rice farms). This ensures competitive and technological superiority.

Agriculture–commerce–industry cooperation, integration, “sextiary sector” approaches, and similar forms of farm management do not merely increase productivity, but also enable the realization of a high value-added agriculture, through the manufacture of processed products and the development of agricultural services (pick-your-own farms, tourist farms, etc.).

Advanced farm management also expands employment. With around 50ha under cultivation, a rice farm subject to this type of management will require part-time and temporary workers. Again, this is not restricted to rice farms. Any farm being managed to produce sales in the 100 million yen bracket will rely a great deal on part-time workers. When we reach the 200–300 million yen bracket, the farms begin to employ full-time workers. Wages are not necessarily high, but the farm’s output will be increased by at least ten million yen per full-time worker, a figure which sufficiently clears the conditions for employing full-time workers among Japan’s farm managers.

In an attempt to ensure opportunities for employment of the elderly, Japan has adopted agricultural policies skewed towards rice farming, for example, artificially maintaining the price of rice. As a result, agriculture has become an unappealing industry: 72% of all of the nation’s rice farms (840,000 households out of 1.17 million in 2010) are in the red and have no prospect of entering the black. The offspring of farming families are not taking over farms from their parents, and new blood is not coming into the industry. The average age of Japan’s farmers, 66 at present, is increasing annually. The discussion above demonstrates that the choice open to us is to discontinue the policy of maintaining the price of rice in order to provide employment in farming villages, and expand employment opportunities by increasing quality and productivity through the introduction of advanced farm management.

Advanced farm management also contributes to increasing the number of farm managers. There are two routes towards the realization of this goal: making farm employees independent, and the fostering of managers by farming families.

Farm employees can be made independent by allowing an employee who has displayed ability on a farm to establish a separate business under the farm’s name, or by establishing an employee education function which aims from the beginning to make employees independent. There is an increasing trend in the area of advanced farm management towards the establishment of systems of education to foster management successors. It has been indicated that it is difficult to develop from a traditional farmer into a farm manager, but the number of farmers who are becoming incorporated in production and sales systems which create food chains, with the result that they operate their farms as farm managers, is increasing. In the area of vegetable farming, results are being realized by production management and sales systems; in livestock production, consignment systems are in use. In addition to this, agriculture–commerce–industry cooperation is producing outcomes in this regard, and farm mergers and acquisitions (M&A) are also contributing to the realization of high-productivity farm management.

4 Creating an Environment for the Development of New Agricultural Businesses

Nevertheless, the food chains which are being created by advanced farm management do not yet possess sufficient strength. The system fails to realize its full potential to the extent that it relies on contracts. Advanced farm management in Japan is not yet actively opening up new markets or engaging in product development, to say nothing of working to create export opportunities. The realization of increased productivity relies to a significant extent on the individual efforts of farm managers, and as a result the level of the industry as a whole is not improving. The "sextiary sector" is realizing value-added production, but the scope is not expanding beyond the individual food value chains created by individual farms, and there is little ripple effect on surrounding enterprises. Above all, advanced farms are positioned as maverick operations within the agricultural industry (i.e. the sector defined by the triangle of administration, agricultural cooperatives, and politics); for example, the number of farms under advanced management is not even 1% of all agricultural enterprises.

There are reasons why the mainstream of Japan's agricultural industry confines itself to product-oriented production, beginning with agricultural policy. Every country engages in product-oriented agriculture to a greater or lesser extent, but the situation in Japan is fixed in place by the systems in effect.

For example, in relation to rice there is the Staple Food Act (Act for Stabilization of Supply–Demand and Prices of Staple Food), and in relation to vegetables, meat and flowers there is the Wholesale Market Act. In the area of unpasteurized milk production there is the Act on Interim Measures concerning Compensation Price for Consumers of Milk for Manufacturing Use. All of these systemic measures serve to isolate producers from consumers. In the case of rice, price negotiations on a transaction basis between the National Federation of Agricultural Cooperative Associations and wholesalers; in the wholesale market system, competition within the market; and in the area of unpasteurized milk, milk price negotiations between designated unpasteurized milk producers' bodies and milk product makers, are also functioning to isolate the two sides.

However, changing this structure will be very difficult. This is not merely because the number of advanced farms is low and the system does not possess adequate strength, but also because the main approach of protectionist agricultural policies is to artificially maintain prices by adjusting the level of production. In the cases of rice and unpasteurized milk production in particular, laws systematize the adjustment of production. It is necessary for producers to maintain production at a level at which it can be controlled, and as a result, agricultural production becomes sealed off in its own realm. Having been placed in this position for an extended period, Japan's agricultural sector has succumbed to the delusion that it is independent of changes in the broader social environment, and this has created a culture which refuses to cooperate or engage with other industries, rendering the creation of food chains a difficult matter.

If we give consideration to actual agricultural business, cooperation with other industries including marketing and processing is important not merely in Japan, but throughout the world. The agricultural sector is not a uniquely independent sector in the world of industry; it is involved in food chains, and has an organic relationship with the materials production and supply sectors and the product processing and marketing sectors. I want agriculture to become one of the sectors supporting economic growth in Japan. However, despite the fact that there is a practical transition to advanced farm management underway, Japan's main agricultural sectors remain backward-looking in this area.

In order to realize reforms, we will first need to address protectionist policies, replacing policies focusing on price (artificial maintenance of the price of rice, etc.) with a system of direct payments, and replacing the laws that isolate production from distribution with a system that promotes the creation of food chains. We must also create an environment which makes it possible to build more extensive networks between agriculture and other industries. It will be essential to reconsider the price maintenance system, upgrade distribution networks, and expand the involvement of companies from outside the industry in agriculture, and it will be necessary to reform the policy environment in order to do so.

Note

1. The "sextiary sector" (sometimes called the "sixth sector") is a Japanese term referring to the diversification of agriculture into agriculture-related manufacturing and services such as food processing and restaurant management. The concept of a "sixth sector" originates from the idea of combining agricultural production (Primary industry: 1) with processing (Secondary industry: 2) and distribution and sales (Tertiary industry: 3) to generate a synergistic relationship ($1 \times 2 \times 3 = 6$).

CHAPTER 3

Japan's Agricultural Policy: Escaping the *Ancien Régime*

Kazuhito Yamashita

Abstract In Japan, high rice prices, supported by Japan's agricultural cooperatives (JAs) and realized by acreage reduction programs that subsidize farmers to cultivate products other than rice for human consumption, have enabled small-scale, inefficient part-time farmers to survive. Income earned by part-time farmers in non-agricultural jobs is deposited with the JA Bank, making it Japan's second-largest bank. The Abe administration initiated reforms of JA but has made no significant gains. Instead, the administration has increased acreage reduction subsidies for fodder rice. This will substantially reduce imports of US corn. If the USA were to bring a dispute to the WTO, it would be allowed to apply retaliatory tariffs to cars imported from Japan. This could lead to the abolition of the acreage reduction policy.

Keywords High rice prices • Part-time farmers • The acreage reduction program • Japan's agricultural cooperatives • The Abe administration • Fodder rice: imports of corn from the USA • The WTO • Retaliatory tariffs • Direct payments

K. Yamashita (✉)
The Canon Institute for Global Studies, Tokyo, Japan

T. Hatta (ed.), *Economic Challenges Facing Japan's Regional Areas*,
https://doi.org/10.1007/978-981-10-7110-2_3

1 Factors in the Decline of Japan's Agriculture

Japan's agriculture is in decline. This decline is particularly conspicuous in the case of rice agriculture. Rice farms account for 70% of Japan's farms, but they produce only 20% of the nation's agricultural output. This fact serves to demonstrate that rice agriculture in Japan is being conducted by small-scale and inefficient farms.

The attempt to ensure farming incomes through manipulation of the price of rice is a particular characteristic of Japan's postwar agricultural policy. From the 1960s onwards, Japan's Agricultural Cooperatives (JAs) launched a major political push in relation to rice prices under the Food Control System, which saw the government purchase rice from farmers. Pressed by the JAs, which were organizing the farming villages that provided a support base to the Liberal Democratic Party (LDP), the government and the ruling party increased rice prices.

Since the scrapping of the Food Control System in 1995, high rice prices have been maintained by the acreage reduction program. Under the program, farmers are paid subsidies to reduce their rice production in order to increase the price of rice. Taxpayers bear a burden of 400 billion yen for these subsidies. In addition, high rice prices mean that consumers bear a burden of 600 billion yen. The scale of Japan's rice production is two trillion yen, and the nation's citizens bear a burden of one trillion yen.

High rice prices have had a negative impact on rice agriculture. High prices have enabled high-cost, small-scale part-time farmers who should have retired from the industry to continue to produce rice. These farmers will not relinquish their land, making it difficult for full-time farmers attempting to live exclusively by farming to obtain land and increase the scale of their operations, thus reducing costs and increasing profits.

Japan's JAs work to maintain high rice prices and keep the acreage reduction program in place. Despite the fact that they are organizations formed by farmers to enable agricultural chemicals and other farming supplies to be purchased at low cost, JAs have exploited the fact that the Anti-Monopoly Act does not apply to them in order to push supplies including fertilizers, agricultural chemicals, farm machinery, and animal feed onto farmers for as much as twice the amount paid in the USA. Naturally, this has also increased the prices of agricultural products.

The high prices of farming supplies and agricultural products mean that the JAs that sell them are able to collect a proportionally high revenue from sales commissions. High tariffs are necessary in order to maintain the prices of agricultural products at levels higher than international prices.

2 The Reasons Agricultural Cooperatives Are Committed to High Rice Prices

Against the background of postwar food shortages, the agricultural cooperative system was formed in order to facilitate the collection of rice from farms by the government. JAs represented an updated version of the wartime agricultural control bodies which had managed all agricultural procedures, from financing to the collection of farm produce, before the war. Because of this, the JAs were permitted to conduct banking services as well as other business operations, a privilege not extended to any other corporate entities in Japan; in addition, despite the fact that they should have functioned as farmers' professional organizations, any resident of an Agricultural Cooperative's region of jurisdiction could become an associate member of the cooperative and utilize any cooperative services such as banking. Later, Agricultural Cooperatives were also granted permission to engage in life and non-life insurance business. As a result, they became corporate entities spanning an unprecedentedly broad range of activities.

From 1955, farming incomes largely stagnated (Fig. 3.1). Large numbers of rice farmers had become part-time farmers, and from the latter half of the 1960s, non-farming incomes began to exceed farming incomes. The aging of farming families without successors also continued, and pension income increased with age.

Incomes from non-agricultural jobs and pensions, in addition to profits from the diversion of agricultural land to non-agricultural uses, which amounts to several trillion yen per year, is deposited with JAs, which also function as banks. The total amount of deposits with JAs has reached 100 trillion yen, making them collectively the second-largest mega-bank in Japan.

Because agriculture is declining, only 1–2% of the funds held by JAs are loaned for agricultural purposes. JAs encourage local people to become associate members, and 30% of the funds deposited with them are loaned to associate members as housing, car, or education loans, or to former

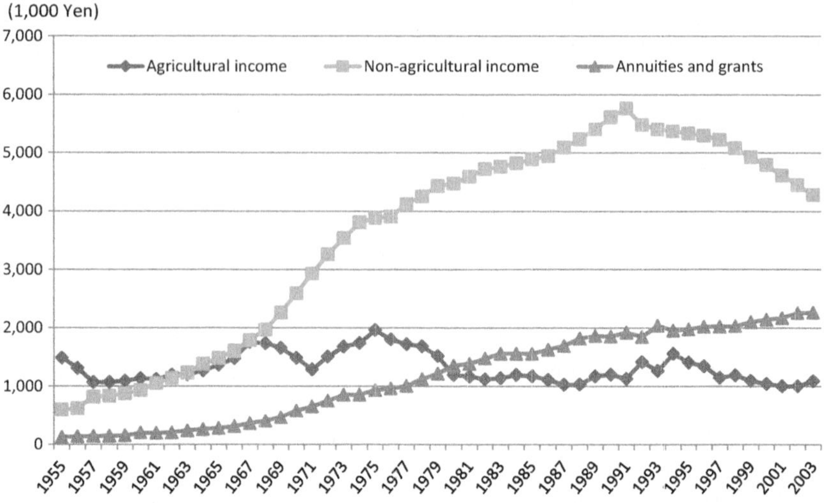

Fig. 3.1 Changes in the breakdown of farming income (1955–2003). Note: Actual figures for 2005, using the GDP deflator from national accounts. Source: Formulated based on Statistical Survey on Farm Management and Economy, Ministry of Agriculture, Forestry and Fisheries, each year (in Japanese)

farm families, for example for the construction of apartments. The remaining 70% of the funds are invested on Wall Street by the Norinchukin Bank, the national organization of the JA banks. Active recruitment of local people has seen the number of associate members of agricultural cooperatives increase annually, turning them into "agriculture–business" cooperatives in which there are as many as 1.5 million more non-farming associate members than regular members. Increasing the price of rice has set all gears turning in harmony for Japan's agricultural cooperatives.

Thus, organizations which were created in order to develop agriculture have actually developed themselves by promoting the decline of agriculture. The abolition of tariffs by the Trans-Pacific Partnership (TPP), resulting in a reduction in the price of rice and the withdrawal from the industry of inefficient part-time farmers and the realization of an agriculture dominated by full-time farmers, would be a massive event which would shake the foundations of the agricultural cooperatives. This is why they have mounted a movement to protest the TPP which has collected more than eleven million signatures.

Every country has bodies which engage in political activities in the cause of agriculture, but only Japan's JAs also engage in economic activities. However, the political and economic interests of JAs are directly linked to the maintenance of high prices. No pressure groups in the USA or the European Union (EU) are fixated on commodity prices in this way.

3 Reform of Agricultural Cooperatives under Abenomics

After 70 years largely without external interference, reform finally came to JAs, collectively the nation's largest postwar pressure group, in 2015.

In May 2014, the government's Regulatory Reform Council formulated a draft proposal for the reform of JAs.

First, provisions concerning the National Union of Agricultural Cooperatives (*Zenchu*) and the Unions of Agricultural Co-operatives in each of the nation's prefectures, which have played the central role in the political activities of the agricultural cooperatives, are to be removed from the Agricultural Cooperatives Act. The *Zenchu* and the prefectural Unions have levied large sums from members. Without the backing of the Agricultural Cooperatives Act, these organizations will be unable to levy mandatory contributions and to control the agricultural cooperatives under their umbrella by means of compulsory audits.

Second, the National Federation of Agricultural Cooperative Associations (*Zennoh*), the Hokuren Group, and other organizations responsible for functions such as the sale of agricultural produce would be transformed into joint stock companies. Agricultural cooperatives are an immense business entity, holding an 80% share of fertilizer sales and a 60% share of agricultural chemical and agricultural machinery sales, chiefly through *Zennoh*, but despite this, as cooperative associations they are not subject to the Anti-Monopoly Act. In addition, they are granted preferential treatment in a variety of areas, including low corporate tax and exemption from fixed assets tax.

The following month, these proposals were watered down by the LDP, based on the response from JAs. However, at the urging of Prime Minister Abe, negotiations were once again opened with JAs, and as a result it was ultimately decided that provisions concerning the *Zenchu* would be removed from the Agricultural Cooperatives Act, the *Zenchu* would become a normal incorporated association like the Keidanren, and regional agricultural cooperatives would be able to choose auditors who were independent of the *Zenchu,* while the prefectural Unions would continue to be covered by the provisions of the Agricultural Cooperatives Act.

This can be expected to weaken the control of the *Zenchu* over regional agricultural associations. However, the prefectural Unions will remain unaltered, and will still be able to levy compulsory contributions. Because the prefectural Unions are members of the *Zenchu*, the contributions they collect will continue to flow to the *Zenchu*, and there may be no change in that organization's political power.

The decision regarding the change of *Zennoh* and other organizations to joint stock companies has been left up to the organizations concerned. Given the greater benefits associated with the status of cooperatives, it is unlikely that they will choose to be joint stock companies.

Ultimately, the current JAs should be kept on as regional cooperatives responsible for providing loans or insurance and supplying basic necessities to local people, and JAs' agricultural divisions should either be disbanded or their functions transferred to new, voluntarily created agricultural cooperatives by full-time farmers. Agricultural cooperatives would be established by full-time farmers as necessary, making them cooperatives in the true sense of the term. With this, reform of the agricultural cooperatives would be complete.

4 Realization of Increased Production of Fodder Rice through Re-examination of the Acreage Reduction System

When it returned to power, the LDP re-examined the acreage reduction policy and scrapped the Income Support Direct Payment Program introduced by the Democratic Party of Japan (DPJ) in 2010. The funds which became available were used to increase the subsidies for the production of rice flour and fodder rice previously introduced by the LDP during its last term in power (the 2009 harvest season). The subsidy was increased to revenue from the sale of rice for direct human consumption use in the 2013 harvest year. A 12,000 yen subsidy called the Growing Region Subsidy was also offered, making the total subsidy provided 117,000 yen per 0.1 hectare. Naturally, growers also received income from the sale of rice flour and fodder rice (Fig. 3.2).

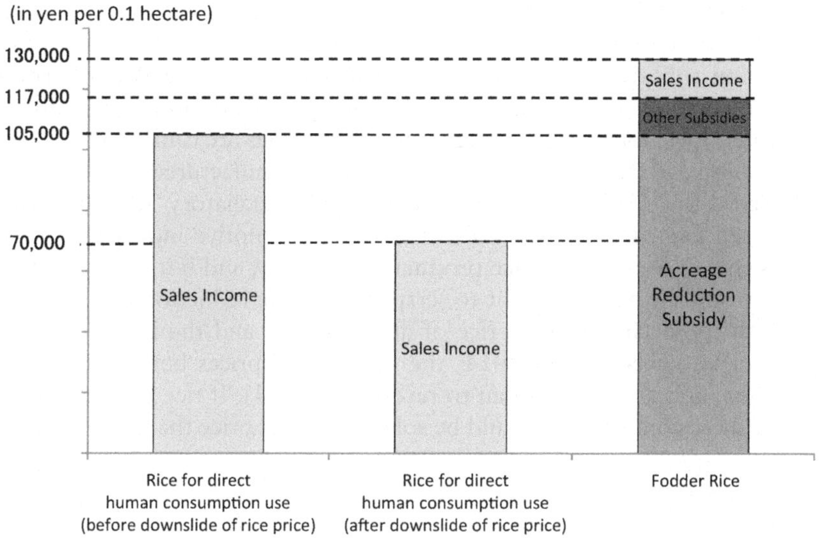

Fig. 3.2 Revenue from production of rice for direct human consumption use and fodder rice. Source: Formulated based on information on rice prices, average rice production volumes and etc. by Ministry of Agriculture, Forestry and Fisheries

If farmers produced rice flour and fodder rice, subsidies alone enabled them to earn revenue in excess of the price of rice in the 2013 harvest year. Revenue from the sale of rice for direct human consumption use fell to 70,000 yen in the 2014 harvest year. Given this, it is clearly advantageous for growers to produce rice flour and fodder rice.

Zennoh purchased 200,000 tons of 2014 fodder rice, but has already planned to triple that amount for rice produced in 2015, to 600,000 tons. If growers expand their production of fodder rice and rice for flour, then the production of rice for direct human consumption use will decline by this amount, and price increases will place pressure on the household budgets of low-income consumers. In addition, the total amount of acreage reduction subsidies will increase, resulting in an increased burden on taxpayers.

The production of high volumes of fodder rice and rice flour would significantly reduce imports of corn and wheat from the USA. Disputes can be brought to the World Trade Organization (WTO) concerning the provision of subsidies of even 5% of selling price. The acreage reduction subsidy for the production of rice for flour and fodder rice corresponds to more than 100% of the price of rice for direct human consumption use. If the USA were to bring a dispute to the WTO in relation to Japan's acreage reduction subsidy, it would certainly win. Given that the WTO permits cross-retaliation (the application of retaliatory tariffs to products in different categories; for example, if agricultural subsidies are causing issues, the application of tariffs to non-agricultural manufactured products is allowed), the USA would be able to apply retaliatory tariffs to cars imported from Japan. The scale of Japan's automotive industry is seven times that of the nation's rice production industry, and if it were affected, there would be no choice but to scrap the acreage reduction policy.

With the decline in the price of domestic rice and the increase in the price of imported rice in 2014, the disparity in prices between the two vanished, and the trend began to reverse (Fig. 3.3). If rice were exported under these conditions, it could be sold at a higher price than the domestic

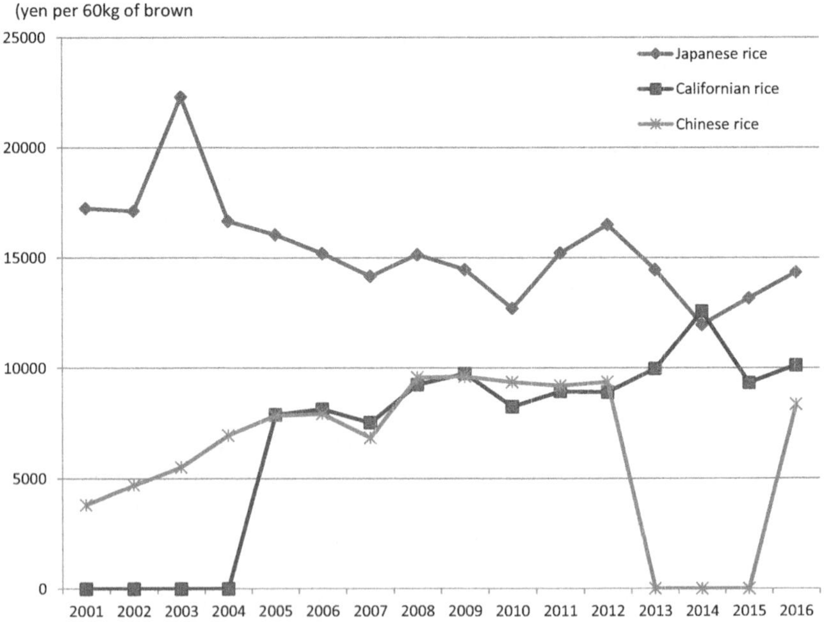

Fig. 3.3 Comparisons of Japanese rice price in the domestic market and purchase price of Californian and Chinese rice under the tariff rate quota for direct human consumption use. Source: Formulated based on documents published by the Ministry of Agriculture, Forestry and Fisheries

price. There would therefore be no need to engage in acreage reduction in order to maintain domestic prices at a lower level than international prices. If the acreage reduction system were scrapped, the domestic price of rice would fall by around 8000 yen per 60 kilograms, enabling large-scale export. If exports increased, then the volume of supply to the domestic market would be reduced, and this would increase the price of rice. If the export price were 12,000 yen per 60 kg, the domestic price of rice would increase to the same level, and domestic rice production would increase.

Over the short term, it would be possible to pay full-time farmers affected by the decline in the price of rice directly from public finances. The 400 billion yen freed up by the scrapping of acreage reduction subsidies would make sufficient funds available. These direct payments would become unnecessary when rice prices increased. In addition, the decline in the price of rice would mean that small-scale part-time farmers, unable to cover their high costs, would quit farming and lease their land to full-time farmers. The ability of these full-time farmers to cover rents would be increased by direct payments from the government, and they would accumulate land, enabling them to expand the scale of their operations and reduce costs. The acreage reduction program forbids varietal improvements which would increase yields, and at present yield per unit area for Japanese rice is 60% lower than it is for Californian rice. Because cost is calculated by dividing cost per unit area by yield per unit area, increasing yield per unit area by scrapping the acreage reduction program would reduce costs. Increasing the scale of farms and increasing yields would significantly boost the price competitiveness of Japanese rice.

Despite being protected by high tariffs, Japan's domestic market is shrinking as a result of the decline in the nation's population. The realization of greater price competitiveness for high-quality Japanese rice through the scrapping of the acreage reduction program would not only render tariffs unnecessary, but would also open up export markets throughout the world. This will be the key to the revitalization of Japanese agriculture.

PART II

Regulatory Reforms: Fishing Policy

CHAPTER 4

Fishing Policy: Toward Introduction of Science-based Measurement/Management of Resources

Masayuki Komatsu

Abstract There have been no substantive amendments to Japan's Fisheries Act since the end of the Second World War, with the result that Japan's fisheries have consistently been allowed to operate under a system of "Olympic-style" fishing. This has caused the decline of fisheries resources and the fishing industry itself, contributing to economic decline in the nation's rural areas (Komatsu 2014). Other major fishing nations have reformed their fisheries-related laws and regulations and spurred growth in their fishing industries. It is essential for the revitalization of Japan's rural areas that we learn from these efforts and rebuild resources, attract external investment, and promote employment.

This chapter discusses the introduction of an individual quota (IQ) system in Niigata Prefecture, and considers fisheries reform attempts proposed by municipalities in Hokkaido.

Keywords Olympic-style fishing • Fisheries Act • Revitalization of rural areas • Individual quota • Niigata Prefecture • Hokkaido

M. Komatsu (✉)
The Tokyo Foundation, Tokyo, Japan

T. Hatta (ed.), *Economic Challenges Facing Japan's Regional Areas*,
https://doi.org/10.1007/978-981-10-7110-2_4

1 Introduction

In the 70 years since the end of the Second World War, the Japanese fisheries have been allowed to operate under a system of "Olympic-style" fishing, in which victory goes to the operator who catches the most fish, due to a lack of amendments to the Fisheries Act and the Fisheries Cooperative Association Act.[1] This has resulted in the decline of fisheries resources and the fisheries, and is a major factor in the decline of rural area economies in Japan (Komatsu, 2011; 2012). Other major fishing nations, including Norway, Iceland, and the USA, have reformed their Fisheries Acts and Regulations and accordingly spurred growth in their fisheries. These nations have succeeded in building fisheries that contribute both to the economies of rural areas and to the economy of the nation as a whole. It is essential for the revitalization of Japan's rural areas that we learn from these efforts and rebuild resources, attract external investment, and promote employment (Japan Economic Research Institute, 2007).

While they have had only limited success, there have been medium- to long-term reform initiatives of the fisheries in Japan. These include the Individual Quota (IQ) system introduced to one Niigata Prefecture shrimp cage fishery, considered in this Section by Kojun Hamada, and the attempts put forward by municipalities on Hokkaido's Rishiri and Rebun Islands, discussed in this chapter by Mari Koyano (Hamada, 2018; Koyano, 2018).[2]

2 The Decline of Japan's Fisheries: The Most Serious Case among OECD Members

Japan's fisheries have displayed the most marked decline among members of the Organization for Economic Co-operation and Development (OECD) (Fig. 4.1).

Japan's deep-sea Fishing Industry has faced the successive imposition of Regulations within coastal nations' 200 nautical mile exclusive economic zones (EEZs), and only a few examples of these industries, such as purse seine fishery operations in the waters of Pacific island nations and deep-sea longline tuna fisheries, remain.

In addition, there has been a conspicuous decline in the volume of catches of fish species within Japan's EEZ. The peak catch of 11.3 million tons for fishing operations within 200 nautical miles of the Japanese coast was taken in 1985; this figure was reduced to 3.53 million tons in 2015 (Fig. 4.2). The coastal fisheries also declined from a catch of 2.10 million

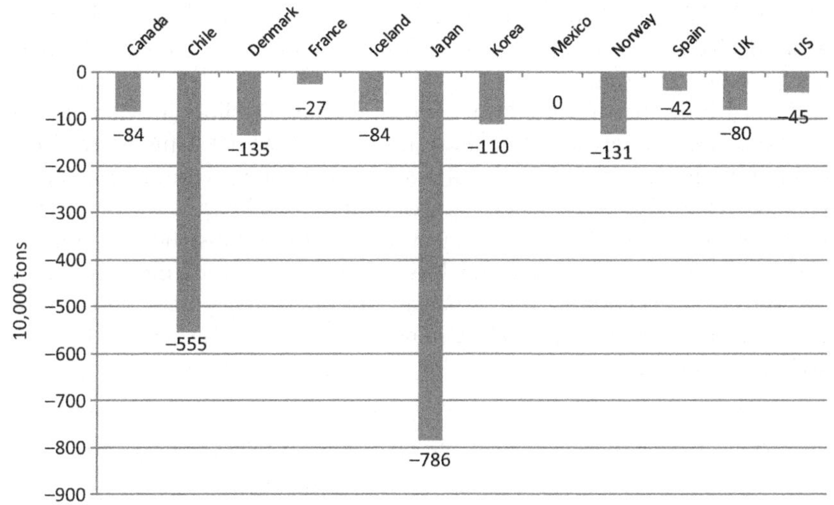

Fig. 4.1 Decline in the fisheries catch between past maximum catch and 2013 catch for OECD member nations with annual catch volumes of 500,000 tons or more. Source: Based on FAO Fishery Statistical Collections, Global Capture Production 1950–2013

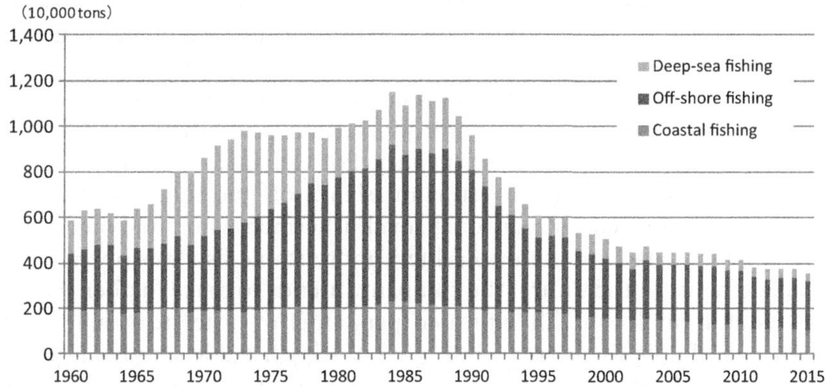

Fig. 4.2 Trends in capture fisheries catch for Japan (1960–2015). Source: Fisheries Statistics by the Ministry of Agriculture, Forestry and Fisheries. 2015 figures are tentative

tons in 1977 to 0.7 million tons in 2015 (excluding scallops, and salmon around Hokkaido, resources of which have increased as a result of hatchery breeding programs).

Overfishing has resulted in a conspicuous Decline in Catches for medium-sized fisheries and offshore fisheries (trawl net fishing, etc.) conducted within Japan's EEZ. Small-scale coastal fisheries and marine aquaculture have also experienced a continuing decline, with the recent reclamation of the lands of coastal waters and the construction of large-scale embankments causing the loss of favorable breeding and fishing grounds in seaweed beds and estuarine and tidal flats, a marked deterioration of fishing grounds, and a lack of new investment in fisheries. Olympic-style fishing is largely responsible for all of these effects.

3 Overseas Success in the Recovery of Fisheries Resources and Fisheries

Almost all of the fisheries products imported by Japan originate in Norway, Iceland, Canada, and the US state of Alaska. All of these have scientifically assessed their fisheries resources, set targets for the sustainable maintenance or recovery of those resources, calculated Available Biological Change (ABC), and set Total Allowable Catch (TAC) below ABC. In addition, they also apply the IQ system, in which the TAC is divided among individual fisheries operators based on criteria including their historical catch volume.

In advanced fisheries nations other than Japan, Individual Transferrable Quotas (ITQs) have been introduced and established, and fisheries businesses have increased their stability. For example, the seafood company VSV, located on the Westmann Islands off the southern coast of Iceland, was formed by individual small fishermen who combined their investments, enabling them to achieve more stable fisheries operational management. In the future, the company intends to make further investments and employ highly educated personnel in order to enable it to reduce its simple workforce while also ensuring a stable supply of fish to the market. It also plans to rationalize the management of its fisheries business.

The Individual Vessel Quota (IVQ) introduced by Norway in 1990 has also produced positive outcomes. The government of Norway is now considering reforms to promote the further stability of the quota management scheme over the next 20 years. They concluded at the committee in

December 2016 and still consider at the Government. Like oil resources, fisheries resources are regarded as common resources among the people living in Norway, and the country is examining the possibility of introducing resource rent and transferability of catch quotas for the smallest category of fishers.

4 New Initiatives in Japan: The Cases of Niigata Prefecture and Hokkaido's Rishiri and Rebun Islands

There are some examples of pioneering efforts within Japan itself. An IQ has been introduced in Niigata Prefecture. On Hokkaido's Rishiri and Rebun Islands, municipalities are pushing ahead with improvements in existing systems, looking towards the renewal and revitalization of the fisheries. Miyagi Prefecture's special fisheries rights initiative, which is intended to extend the rights to aquaculture fisheries to private companies, rather than limiting them to the fishermen who are members of fisheries cooperative associations, is another example of a new initiative to reform the Fisheries Act of Japan. These initiatives have yet to progress, and their success remains limited, but as a starting point for reform efforts in Japan, it is to be hoped that they will inspire further efforts on a national basis. Since Niigata Prefecture introduced its model IQ program in FY 2011, the revenue of operators participating in the program (shrimp pot fishing of sweet shrimp, *Pandalus eous*) has seen a rapid and significant improvement (Fig. 4.3) (Komatsu, 2015; Niigata Prefecture, 2011).

In Chap. 5, Associate Professor Kojun Hamada analyzes the economic effect of the establishment of this model IQ program in terms of an increase in the price of fishery products, and discusses the benefits of the introduction of IQ (Hamada, 2018). It is of considerable interest that these benefits do not accrue only to participants in the specific fisheries to which the IQ was introduced; the IQ also has an economic ripple effect on other fishing industries catching the same species.

Based on actual field surveys, in Chap. 6 Professor Mari Koyano offers a consideration, from a legal perspective, of current initiatives being conducted on Hokkaido's Rishiri and Rebun Islands, elucidating the basis for efforts to manage sea cucumbers, sea urchins, and other important coastal resources (Koyano, 2018). Together, these chapters can be considered to offer a succinct introduction to current efforts to promote recovery in Japan's fisheries resources.

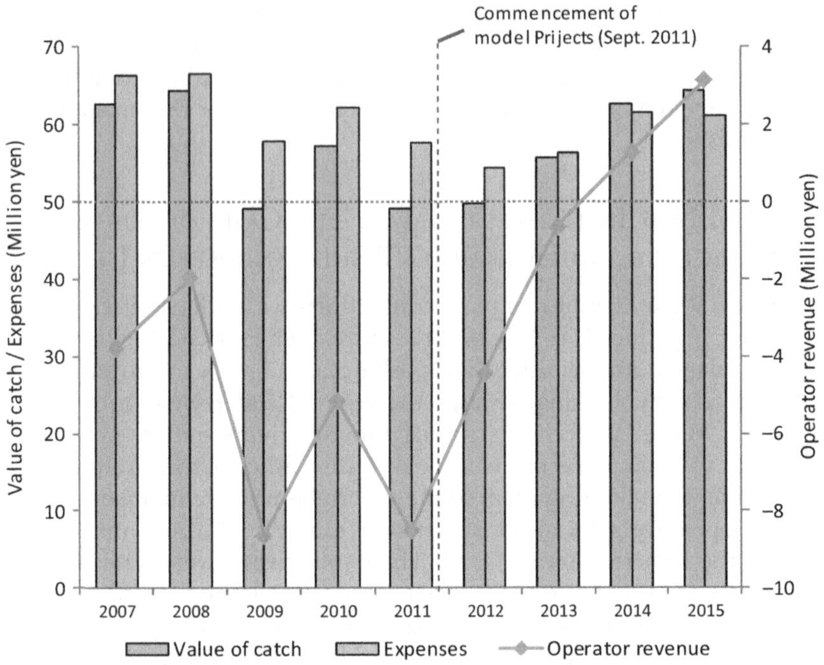

Fig. 4.3 Trends in revenue among participants in Niigata Prefecture's model IQ fishery. Source: "Document 5," 8th Niigata Prefecture Committee for Overall Evaluation of New Resource Management (Convened on July 26, 2016)

Notes

1. "Olympic-style" fishing refers to a system in which neither a fishing period nor a total catch volume is set for the purpose of resource management, or even if a total allowable catch (TAC) is set, it may not be allotted as an individual quota to each operator or boat. This system favors operators who catch the most fish in the shortest amount of time, hence the term "Olympic-style." "Olympic-style" fishing has a negative effect on resources, because it encourages operators to catch even juvenile fish, despite their low market price. The administrative authorities in Japan tend to set the TAC based on socioeconomic factors beyond the scientifically verified allowable biological catch (ABC).
2. Individual quota, or IQ, is allotted to individual operators (or individual boats) based on historical catches within the TAC. Because operators must stay within their allotted quotas, IQ leads them to closely follow market

needs and trends, avoiding lower-priced juvenile fish and selectively catching larger fish. This has the benefit of both increasing operators' income and protecting fisheries resources.

References

Hamada, Kojun (2018), "Introduction of an Individual Quota (IQ) System to Japan's Fishing Industry: An Economic Analysis," in T. Hatta (ed.), *Economic Challenges Facing Japan's Regional Areas*, Plagrave Macmillan, pp. 39–49.

Japan Economic Research Institute (2007), *Gyoshoku wo Mamoru Suisangyo no Senryakutekina Bapponkaikaku wo Isoge* (Accelerating Fundamental Strategic Reform of Japan's Fishing Industry to Protect the Nation's Fish-eating Culture), Research Paper of Takagi Fishing Industry Reform Committee. (In Japanese)

Komatsu, Masayuki (2011), *Umi wa Darenomono ka* (Who Owns the Sea?), Magazine Land. (In Japanese)

Komatsu, Masayuki (2012), *Who Owns the Sea?*, The Japan Times.

Komatsu, Masayuki (2014), *Nihon no Umikara Sakana ga Kieruhi* (When the Fish Disappear from Japan's Waters), Magazine Land. (In Japanese)

Komatsu, Masayuki (2015), "The Reform of Japan's Fisheries. Does Individual Quota Contribute to Inclusive Innovation and Innovative Management?," International Conference of Inclusive Innovation and Innovative Management (ICIIIM 2015)

Koyano, Mari (2018), "Revitalization of Japan's Fishing Industry: A Legal Perspective—The Case of Rishiri and Rebun Island," in T. Hatta (ed.), *Economic Challenges Facing Japan's Regional Areas*, Plagrave Macmillan, pp. 51–64.

Niigata Prefecture (2011), Niigataken Shinshigenseido Dounyukentoiinkai Hokokusho (Report of the Niigata Prefecture Committee for the Review of the Introduction of New Resource Management Systems), September 2011. (In Japanese)

CHAPTER 5

Introduction of an Individual Quota (IQ) System to Japan's Fishing Industry: An Economic Analysis

Kojun Hamada

Abstract Individual quota (IQ) systems are effective methods of management of fisheries resources and are being implemented by nations throughout the world. Japan's first IQ system was introduced to the Alaskan pink shrimp pot fishery in the Akadomari region of Sado Island. This chapter examines the resulting change in the unit prices of the shrimp shipped from this shrimp pot fishery. The results demonstrate that by reducing competition with the trawl net fishery and allowing operation during summer, the introduction of an IQ system realized the advantage of enabling shipments of shrimp during the high-price, high-demand period. The IQ system offers shrimp pot fishers an economic incentive to catch and ship as much as possible of their allotted volume of shrimp in the highest-priced period.

Keywords Individual quota (IQ) system • Japan's fishing industry • Shrimp pot fishery • Alaskan pink shrimp • Market price • Avoidance of competition • Economic incentive

K. Hamada (✉)
Faculty of Economics, Niigata University, Niigata, Japan

T. Hatta (ed.), *Economic Challenges Facing Japan's Regional Areas*,
https://doi.org/10.1007/978-981-10-7110-2_5

1 Introduction

The decline of Japan's fishing industry has long been a focus of attention. According to Fisheries Agency data, Japan's catch has been steadily declining since its peak in 1984 (see Ministry of Agriculture, Forestry and Fisheries). The depletion of the nation's fisheries resources by overfishing is considered to be a factor in the decline of Japan's fishing industry.[1] By contrast, in nations such as Iceland and Norway, which have implemented policies for the appropriate management of their fisheries resources, the fishing industry is a growth industry. In order to prevent overfishing and maintain its fisheries resources, it will be essential for Japan to implement effective resource management measures. The individual quota (IQ) system is available as a method of effective management of fisheries resources, and it is one that is being implemented by nations throughout the world. Individual quotas enable management of fisheries resources by allotting a specific annual catch volume to each fishery operator or each vessel; exceeding the allotted catch volume is prohibited. Because the allotted catch is regulated, fisheries resources do not experience the tragedy of the commons. In addition, because the system allows fishery operators to take their allotted catch at any time, they are able to bring fish to the market when the price is highest, enabling economically rational operation.[2]

Japan's first real IQ system was introduced in 2011, targeting shrimp pot fishing of Alaskan pink shrimp in the Akadomari area of Sado Island, in Niigata Prefecture.[3] This chapter conducts a comparison of market prices of Alaskan pink shrimp before and after the introduction of the IQ system in the Sado Island fishery to study changes in market prices and to determine whether the system is economically rational.

2 Merits and Demerits of IQ Systems

IQ systems can be considered to possess two main merits. The first of these is the fact that allotting each fishery operator a fixed catch does away with "Olympic fishing," the competition to catch the most fish as quickly as possible. The second is that the system generates an economic incentive to catch the fish with the minimum expense and bring them to market at the highest price, thus promoting efficient operations. The demerits of the system are the potential for concealment and false reporting by operators who exceed their quota, and the issue of how to determine the quota itself. However, these demerits can be overcome by appropriate checking of the volume of fish brought to market, and by calculating the allocated quotas based on scientific measurement and management of the actual fishery resources. Major fishing nations such as Iceland and Norway have introduced IQ systems to considerable success.

3 A Comparison of the Unit Price of Alaskan Pink Shrimp Before and After the Introduction of the Akadomari IQ System

The year 2016 marked the sixth year since the introduction of an IQ system to the shrimp pot fishing industry of Akadomari on Sado Island. This section compares the market prices of Alaskan pink shrimp under major brand names before and after the introduction of this groundbreaking system in order to gauge its economic effects. Figure 5.1 shows a scatter

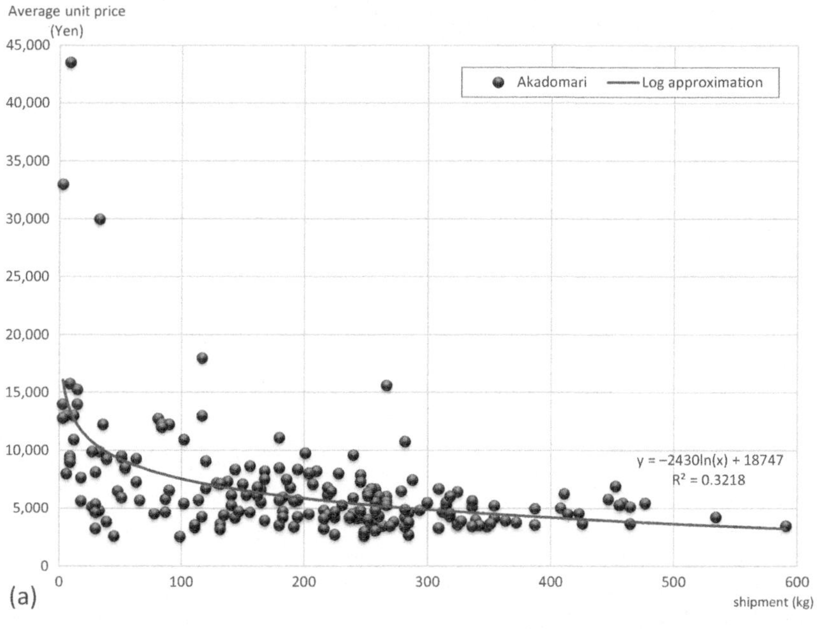

Fig. 5.1 Scatter diagrams of prices before and after introduction of IQ system (Comparison for FY 2010, 2013, and 2014). (a) Before introduction of IQ system (FY 2010). (b) First year of introduction of IQ system (2013). (c) Second year of introduction of IQ system (2014). Source: Based on "Document 4," 8th Niigata Prefecture Comprehensive Evaluation Committee for New Resource Management System (Convened on July 26, 2016)

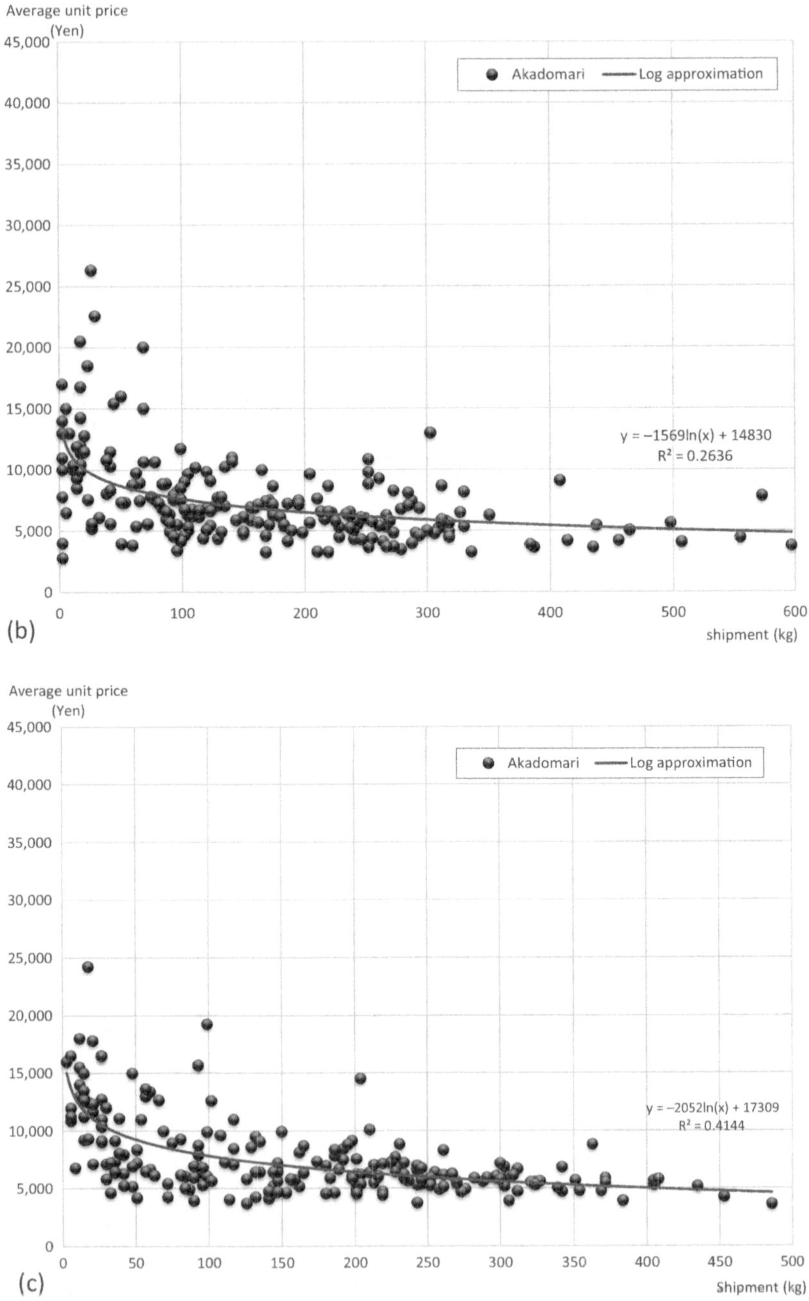

Fig. 5.1 (Continued)

diagram of the volume of shipments of Alaskan pink shrimp from Sado Island under major brand names and unit prices of the shrimp before and after the introduction of the IQ system.

While three outliers can be observed in Fig. 5.1 before the introduction of the IQ system, overall unit prices of shipments of shrimp from Sado Island have tended to increase since the introduction of the system. Figure 5.2 shows a graph of changes in the average unit prices of shipments from Sado Island, as calculated from this market price data.

Figure 5.2 shows that average unit prices have increased following the introduction of the IQ system. The average unit price of shipments from Sado Island was 6711 yen per box in FY 2010, prior to the introduction of the system. This figure increased to 7471 yen per box, an increase of 760 yen per box, in 2013, following the introduction of the IQ system. The unit price increased to 7658 yen per box in 2014, the second year

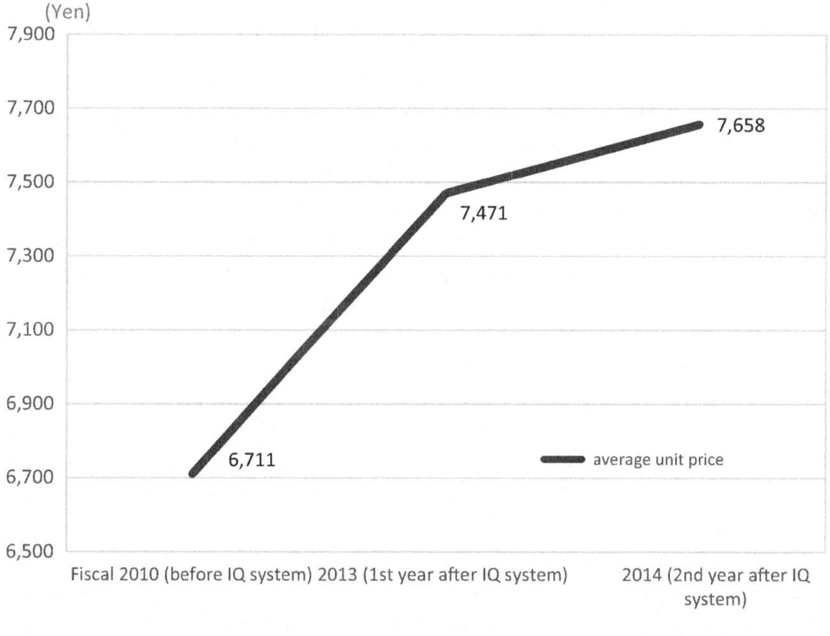

Fig. 5.2 Change in average unit prices following introduction of IQ system. Source: Based on "Document 4," 8th Niigata Prefecture Comprehensive Evaluation Committee for New Resource Management System (Convened on July 26, 2016)

following the introduction of the system, representing a further increase of 187 yen per box, and an increase of 947 yen per box against the average unit price prior to the introduction of the IQ system. These are comparisons of simple averages, but the elimination of the three high outliers prior to the introduction of the system results in a further increase in unit prices.

The fact that the introduction of the IQ system made it possible for shrimp fishers to operate in summer, when unit prices are high, can be considered to be one reason for the increase in average unit prices. In addition, it can also be conjectured that operation in the summer months prevents competition between pot fishing and offshore trawl net fishing, with a consequent increase in the average unit price for the latter. Unit price data by month does show an increase in average unit prices for trawl net fishing in July and August.

4 Effect of Avoidance of Competition in Increasing Unit Prices

One factor causing a decline in prices for Alaskan pink shrimp shipped under major brands was the fact that shrimp caught by shrimp pot operators and shrimp caught by trawl net operators would be shipped to Niigata markets on the same day. Because it allots an annual catch to each fishery operator, the introduction of the IQ system possesses the merit of enabling operators to maximize their profit by choosing the months or weeks when unit prices are highest to make and ship their catch. Here, we investigate whether or not the introduction of the system has made it possible to avoid a decline in unit prices due to market competition.

Figure 5.3 shows a scatter diagram of market prices for shrimp shipped by Sado Island shrimp pot operators when they did and did not compete in the market with shrimp shipped by trawl net operators. Figure 5.4 shows a graph of average unit prices for the Sado Island shrimp pot catch before and after the introduction of the IQ system, calculated from market price data.

A comparison of average unit prices for shipments from Sado Island shrimp pot operators when the shipments compete with shipments from trawl net operators and when they do not, as shown in Fig. 5.4, clearly indicates that average unit prices increase when there is no competition. This verifies the hypothesis that avoidance of competition is

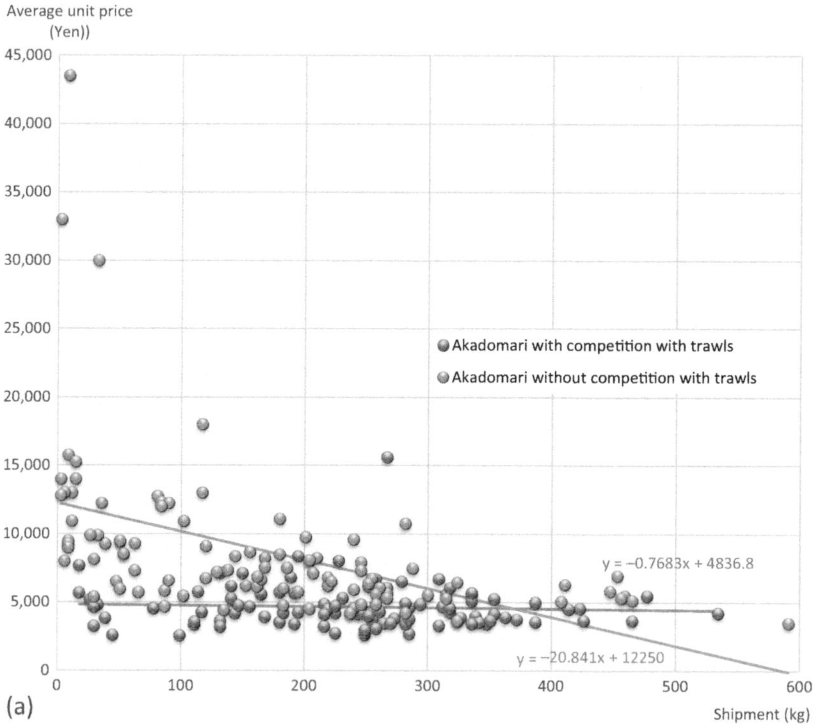

Fig. 5.3 Comparison of unit prices for shipments from Sado Island shrimp pot fishery with and without competition with trawl net fishery before and after introduction of IQ system (Comparison for FY 2010, 2013, and 2014). (a) Before introduction of IQ system (FY 2010). (b) First year of introduction of IQ system (2013). (c) Second year of introduction of IQ system (2014). Source: Based on "Document 4," 8th Niigata Prefecture Comprehensive Evaluation Committee for New Resource Management System (Convened on July 26, 2016)

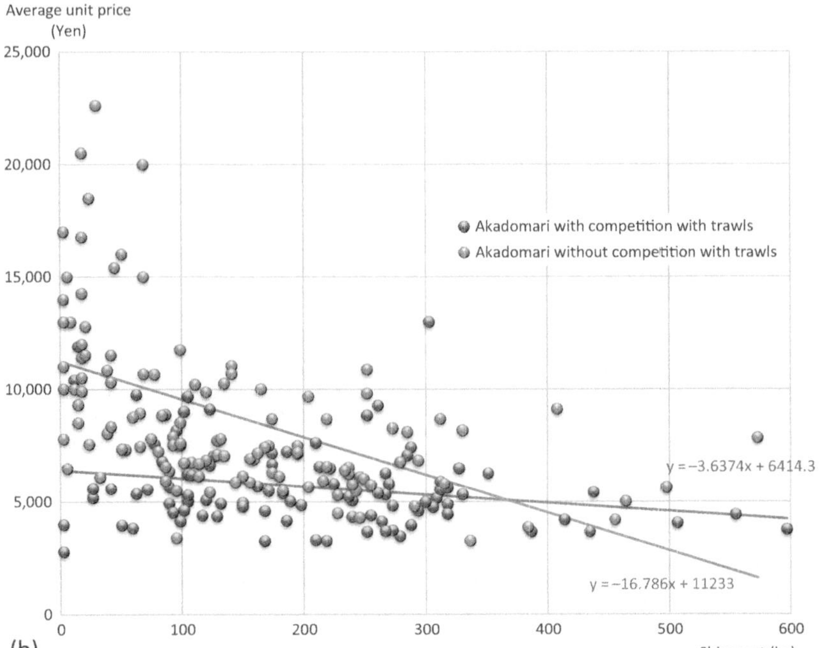

(b)

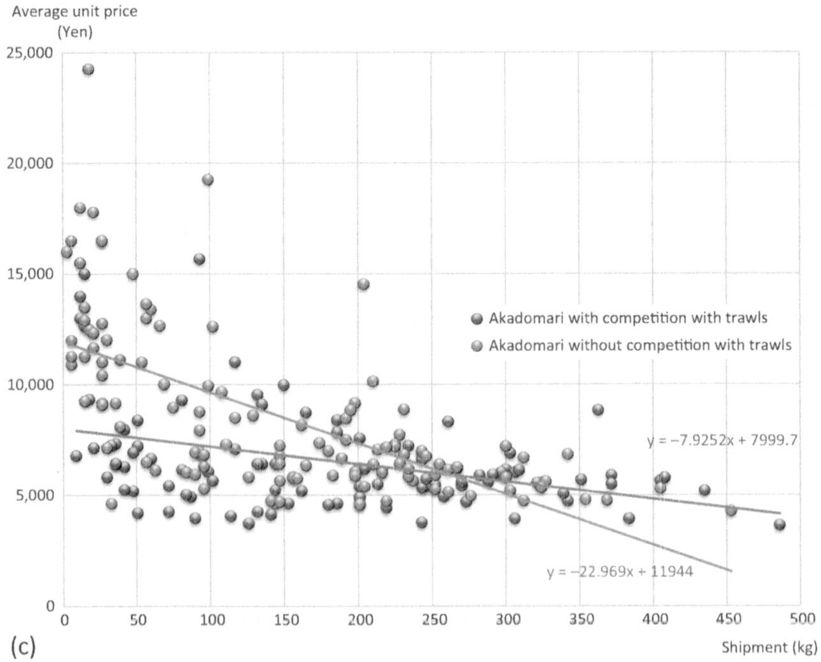

(c)

Fig. 5.3 (Continued)

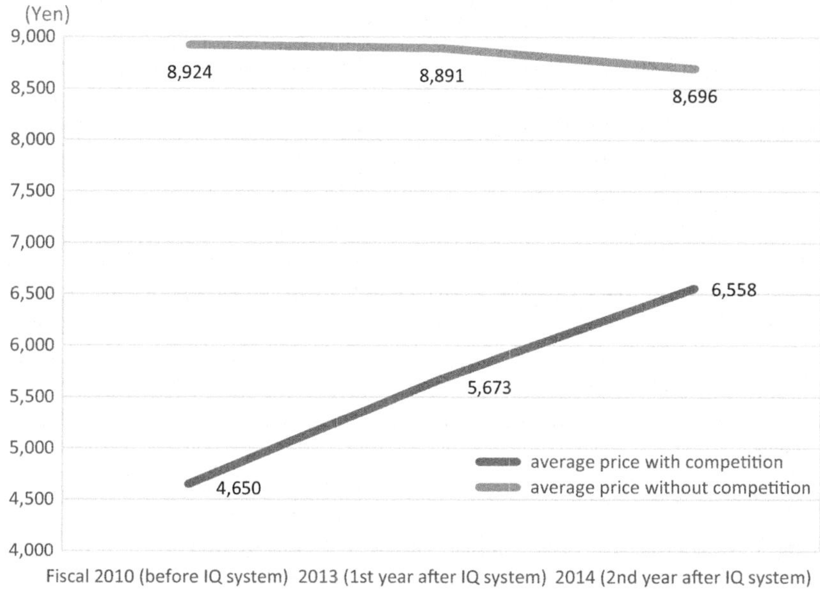

Fig. 5.4 Change in average unit prices for shipments from Sado Island shrimp pot fishery with and without competition with trawl net fishery shipments following introduction of IQ system. Source: Based on "Document 4," 8th Niigata Prefecture Comprehensive Evaluation Committee for New Resource Management System (Convened on July 26, 2016)

linked to a steady increase in unit prices. In terms of the effect of introduction of the IQ system, there is a slight decline in average unit prices when there is no competition following the introduction of the system, but overall not a great deal of change. However, there is a significant increase in average unit prices when there is competition following the introduction of the IQ system. Given that there was almost no change in the actual number of days on which shrimp were shipped following the introduction of the system, it may be conjectured that the number of days of operation and shipment by shrimp pot operators in competition with trawl net operators declined with an increase in the number of days of operation during the summer months (when there is no competition), resulting in increased unit prices when there was competition.

5 Conclusion

This chapter has discussed the results of a study of changes in the unit prices of Alaskan pink shrimp shipped under major brand names from the shrimp pot fishery of the Akadomari region of Sado Island following the introduction of an IQ system in Japan's first attempt at the implementation of such a system. The data indicated that the average unit prices of shrimp shipped from the Sado Island fishery under major brand names tended to increase following the introduction of the system. Data for unit prices of shipments from the Sado Island shrimp pot fishery before the introduction of the system contained three outliers, representing rapid increases in price at the end of the year and during the Golden Week holiday period. When these values were eliminated, the tendency towards increase in unit prices following the introduction of the IQ system became clearer.

Next, the nature of change in the status of competition between shipments from the Sado Island shrimp pot fishery and the offshore trawl net fishery following the introduction of the IQ system was studied in order to determine the reasons for the increase in unit prices following the introduction of the system. The results of this study indicated that following the introduction of the IQ system, there had been a significant increase in the average unit prices of shipments from the shrimp pot fishery when there was market competition with the trawl net fishery, while there had been a slight decline in average unit prices when there was no competition. It is conjectured that the reason for this increase in average unit prices following the introduction of the IQ system was that the introduction of the system had encouraged shrimp pot operation during the summer months, when unit prices were higher, and the number of days in which the shrimp pot catch was in competition with the trawl net catch had decreased as a result of shrimp pot operation in summer.

The results of this study demonstrate that by reducing competition with the trawl net fishery and allowing operation during summer, the introduction of an IQ system to the Sado Island Alaskan pink shrimp pot fishery realized the advantage of enabling shipments during the high-price, high-demand period. The system has the merit of providing fishery operators with an economic incentive to catch and ship as much as possible of their allotted volume of shrimp in the highest-priced period. The results demonstrating an increase in unit prices for shrimp discussed in this chapter provide further support for the economic efficiency of the introduction of IQ systems. In Japan, where the depletion of fishery resources has long been a subject of discussion and the management of these resources is an urgent issue, the further application of IQ systems displaying this type of economic rationality holds great promise as a prescription for the revitalization of the nation's fisheries.

Notes

1. As regarding the recent issues on Japan's fishery, see Komatsu (2014).
2. As a recent study, Takarada and Managi (2010) summarized the effectiveness of IQ system.
3. Komatsu (2015) reported this innovative introduction of IQ system in Japan in detail.

References

Komatsu, Masayuki (2014), "*Interview Nihon no Shoku no Mirai: File2 Gyogyohukkatsu no Shohosen* (Interview: Japan's Food Future (File 2): A Prescription for the Revitalization of Japan's Fishing Industry)," *Nikkei Business Online*, June 10, 11, and 12, 2014. (http://business.nikkeibp.co.jp/article/interview/20140606/266327/) (In Japanese).

Komatsu, Masayuki (2015), "*Niigataken Sadoshima de Nihonhatsu no Honkakuteki 'Kobetsu Gyokaku Wariate Seido' wo Donyu* (Introduction of Japan's First Fully Fledged Individual Quota System on Sado Island, Niigata Prefecture)," Shima, Vol. 60(3), pp. 30–41 (In Japanese).

Ministry of Agriculture, Forestry and Fisheries, *Survey on Marine Fishery Production* (http://www.maff.go.jp/j/tokei/kouhyou/kaimen_gyosei/index.html) (In Japanese).

Takarada, Yasuhiro, and Managi, Shunsuke (2010), *Shigen-keizaigaku eno Shotai: Case study toshiteno Suisangyo* (An Invitation to Resource Economics: Fisheries Case Studies), Minerva Shobo (In Japanese).

CHAPTER 6

Revitalization of Japan's Fishing Industry: A Legal Perspective—The Cases of Rishiri and Rebun Islands

Mari Koyano

Abstract Japan's fishing industry faces two problems: a decline in overall production and catches of key species, and a decline in the number of fishing industry workers and general aging of the population. These problems represent a threat to the sustainability of Hokkaido's fishing industry, the cornerstone of Japan's fishing industry, and of Hokkaido's coastal and offshore island communities. Focusing on Hokkaido's Rishiri and Rebun Islands, this chapter considers legislative and policy perspectives relating to the problem of declining catches. The chapter suggests that the enhancement of fisheries resource management beyond existing voluntary measures, based on scientific data and with respect for the experiences of fishing communities, may be the key to promoting sustainable fisheries and ensuring the survival of the local communities that rely on them.

Keywords Fishing industry • Decline in catches • Sustainable fisheries • Sustainable development of local communities • Hokkaido • Rishiri and

M. Koyano (✉)
Graduate School of Law, The Advanced Institute for Law and Politics Globalisation, Hokkaido University, Hokkaido, Japan

T. Hatta (ed.), *Economic Challenges Facing Japan's Regional Areas*,
https://doi.org/10.1007/978-981-10-7110-2_6

Rebun Islands • Fisheries resource management • Decline in number of fishing industry workers • Aging of the population of fishing industry workers • TAC (total allowable catch) • Cultivation and release of juveniles (sea urchins and sea cucumbers)

1 Introduction

Hokkaido is the cornerstone of Japan's fishing industry. In 2014, production in Hokkaido's marine fishing and aquaculture industries, in terms of both quantity and value, was the highest of any of the nation's prefectures (Hokkaido, 2016). In addition to being one of Hokkaido's key industries, the fishing industry also provides the economic foundation for communities in the prefecture's coastal areas and on its offshore islands. However, like other areas of Japan, Hokkaido faces two problems: a decline in overall production and in catches of key species (walleye pollock, Pacific saury, chum salmon, etc.), and a decline in the number of fishing industry workers and general aging of the population (Hokkaido, 2016). These problems represent a threat to the sustainability of Hokkaido's fishing industry and of the prefecture's regional communities.

Taking the cases of Hokkaido's Rishiri and Rebun Islands as examples, this chapter looks at the problem of declining catches from the legislative and policy perspective. The communities of both islands have historically been extremely reliant on the fishing industry, and the issues of declining catches and aging populations are making themselves felt. Against this background, the town communities on the islands have mounted independent initiatives in relation to fisheries resources, making them ideal to consider as case studies. The labor force and population issues affecting both islands should also be considered, but limitations of space prevent it on this occasion.

2 The Fishing Industries of Rishiri and Rebun Islands

Rishiri and Rebun Islands are located in the Sea of Japan northwest of Hokkaido. The towns of Rishirifuji and Rishiri are located on Rishiri Island, and the town of Rebun is located on Rebun Island (Map 6.1).

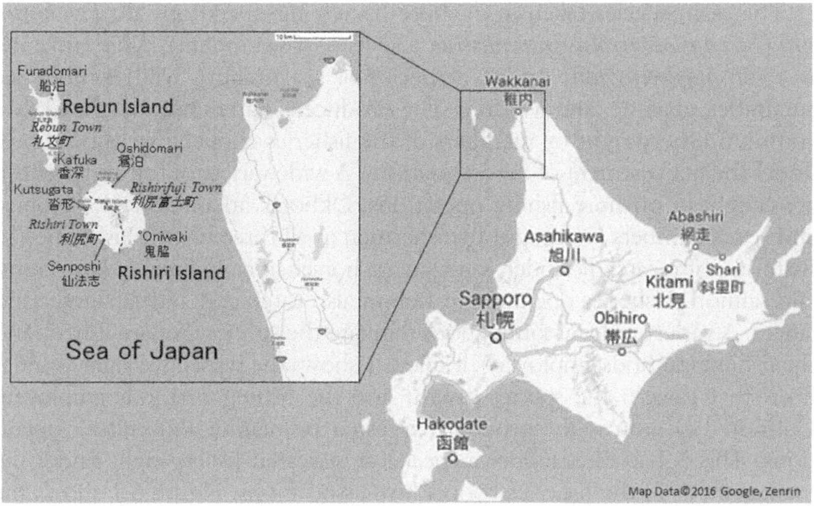

Map 6.1 Location of Rishiri and Rebun Islands. Note: This map was prepared by the author based on Google Maps

The ocean surrounding Rishiri and Rebun Islands offers particularly abundant fishing grounds. The islands lie close to the La Perouse Strait (the Strait of Soya), and are affected by both the intermingling of the cold waters of the Liman Current and the warm waters of the Tsushima Current and drift ice from the Sea of Okhotsk. The waters around the islands were previously rich in herring, and fishing remains the main industry in the islands' towns. This is followed by tourism, but the number of tourists visiting the islands has halved in the past 12 years. Depopulation is severe on the islands, with the populations having declined dramatically since 1955, when there was a poor herring catch. More than 30% of the population of the islands is aged over 65.

With the exception of processing of the catch by the fisheries cooperative association in Funadomari, in Rebun Town, the fishing industry of both islands has traditionally centered on marine fishing. Three types of fishing are practiced on the islands: in-shore harvesting of sea urchin, abalone and so forth; offshore fishing; and marine aquaculture. Almost all fisheries operators on the islands are engaged in in-shore harvesting. There is also considerable offshore fishing activity on Rebun Island.

The main species taken in in-shore harvesting operations are *Ezo-bafun uni* (*Strongylocentrotus intermedius*, a species of sea urchin), *Kita-murasaki uni* (*Strongylocentrotus nudus*, a species of sea urchin), wild kombu, sea cucumber, abalone, and wakame. The produce is harvested under a Class 1 common fishery right by members of the fisheries cooperative associations, under the management of the associations. A wide variety of fish and shellfish are caught in offshore fishing operations. Okhotsk atka mackerel, octopus, and sea cucumbers are caught by fishermen in all three towns. Fishermen in Rishirifuji also catch flounder, sand lances, horsehair crabs and red king crabs, and salmon. Fisheries operators in Rebun also catch cod and Japanese sand lances. A variety of legal foundations regulate the species that are fished (and the fishing methods employed). Table 6.1 shows the respective legal foundations that govern the species caught and the fishing methods employed. Cultivated kombu is the product harvested by marine aquaculture operations. This is harvested under a special demarcated fishery right under the management of the fisheries cooperative associations. Figure 6.1 shows the volume and value of production for the main species caught or harvested.

In recent years, catches of the main species *Ezo-bafun uni* (in in-shore harvesting operations) and Okhotsk atka mackerel and cod (in offshore fishing operations) have been declining (Fig. 6.2). While the reasons for this are not clear, factors including increased water temperature, change in currents, fishing pressure, and a decline in the number of fisheries workers may be involved.

Three fisheries cooperative associations are located on the islands: The Rishiri Fisheries Cooperative Association (formed as an amalgamation of four fisheries cooperative associations (Oshidomari, Oniwaki, Kutsugata, and Senhoshi) in 2008) is based on Rishiri Island, and the Kafuka and Funadomari Fisheries Cooperatives are based on Rebun Island. As of January 2016, the Rishiri Fisheries Cooperative Association had 315 members, the Kafuka Fisheries Cooperative Association had 150 members, and the Funadomari Fisheries Cooperative Association had 210 members. Membership numbers for each cooperative association are in ongoing decline. The highest proportion of cooperative members are in their forties and fifties, and the average age of members is around 65. The cooperative associations are of differing economic scale. According to 2013 data, both amount of sales and balance of savings per member are highest for the Funadomari Fisheries Cooperative Association, with figures twice those for the Rishiri Fisheries Cooperative Association (Hokkaido Government Soya General Subprefectural Bureau, 2015).

Table 6.1 Legal foundations regulating main species caught or harvested on Rishiri and Rebun Islands

Species (Fishing method)	*Legal foundation*
Okhotsk atka mackerel, flounder, Pacific cod (Gill net fishing)	Approved by fisheries cooperative associations based on a Class 2 common fishery right, or, when moving boats are employed, authorized by the Governor based on Article 5 of the Regulations for the Management of Hokkaido's Fisheries (differs depending on the area of operation)
Octopus (Line fishing, use of lights as lures)	Approved by fisheries cooperative associations based on a Class 1 common fishery right, or, when moving boats are employed, authorized by the Governor based on Article 5 of the Regulations for the Management of Hokkaido's Fisheries (differs depending on the area of operation)
Sea cucumber (Trawl fishing)	Both approval by fisheries cooperative associations based on a Class 1 common fishery right and authorization by the Governor based on Article 5 of the Regulations for the Management of Hokkaido's Fisheries are necessary
Sand lance (Lift net fishing by firelight, etc.)	Authorized by the Governor based on Article 5 of the Regulations for the Management of Hokkaido's Fisheries
Sand lance (Skim-net fishing)	Approved by the Soya Fishery Regulation Committee
Sand lance (Small fixed-net fishing)	Approved based on a Class 2 common fishery right
Sand lance (Beach seine netting)	Approved based on a Class 3 common fishery right
Horsehair crab, king crab (Gill-net fishing)	Authorized by the Governor based on Article 45 of the Regulations for the Management of Hokkaido's Fisheries (special harvest[a])
Salmon (Gill-net fishing)	Authorized by the Governor based on Article 45 of the Regulations for the Management of Hokkaido's Fisheries (special harvest[b])

Source: Based on e-mail responses received from the Fisheries Section of the Industry Promotion Department, Soya Regional Development Bureau via the Rishirifuji Town administration on 9 August 2016, from the Rishiri Town administration on 2 August 2016 and from the Rebun Town administration on 1 August 2016.

[a]Surveys are conducted using gill nets in order to study the volume of resources, establish optimal operational systems, and analyze resource distribution and management (the potential for commercialization is being examined)

[b]Surveys of the effectiveness of releasing fry and the number of adult fish returning are conducted using gill nets

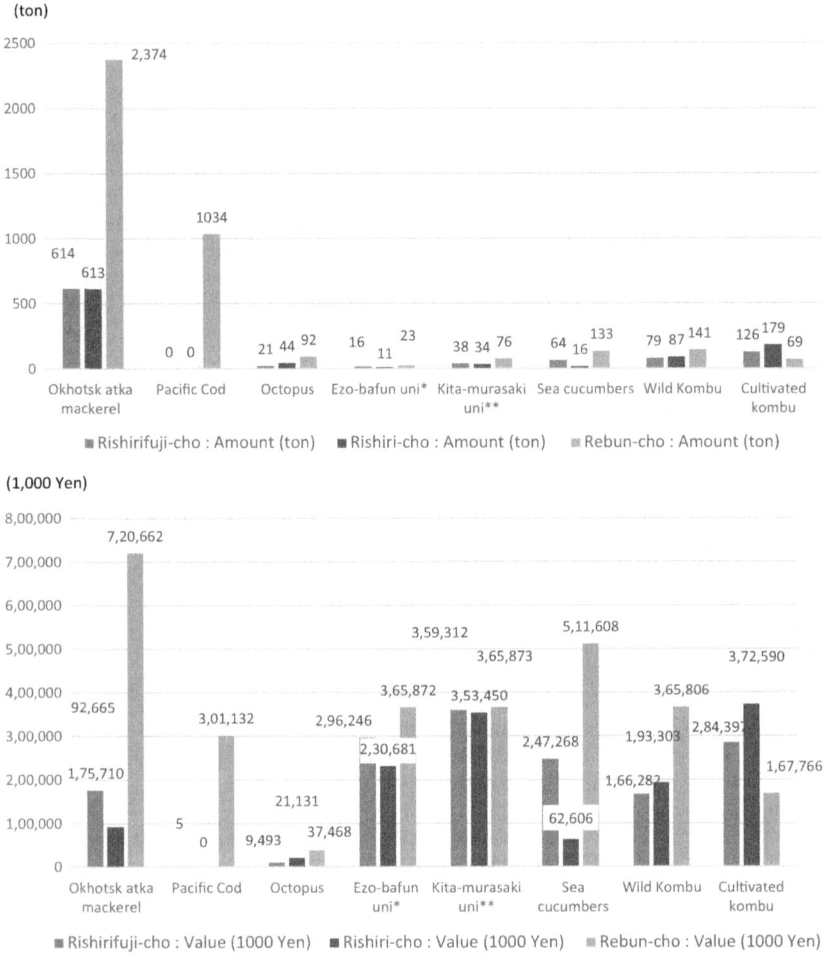

Fig. 6.1 Production for the main species harvested in 2015 at Rishirifuji-cho, Rishiri-cho, and Rebun-cho. (**a**) The volume of production. (**b**) The value of production. * *Strongylocentrotus intermedius*, a species of sea urchin, locally called "Uni." ** *Strongylocentrotus nudus*, a species of sea urchin, locally called "Nona." Source: These figures were prepared by the author based on data in the below referenced materials: Fisheries Ports Administrator, Rishirifuji Town (2016) "Rishirifuji Fisheries, 2016 Edition" (in Japanese); Community Development Department, Rishiri Town (2016) "Documents Relating to Status of Fisheries Production, 2015" (in Japanese); and Rebun Town (2016) "Trends in Fishery Yields, by Species" (in Japanese)

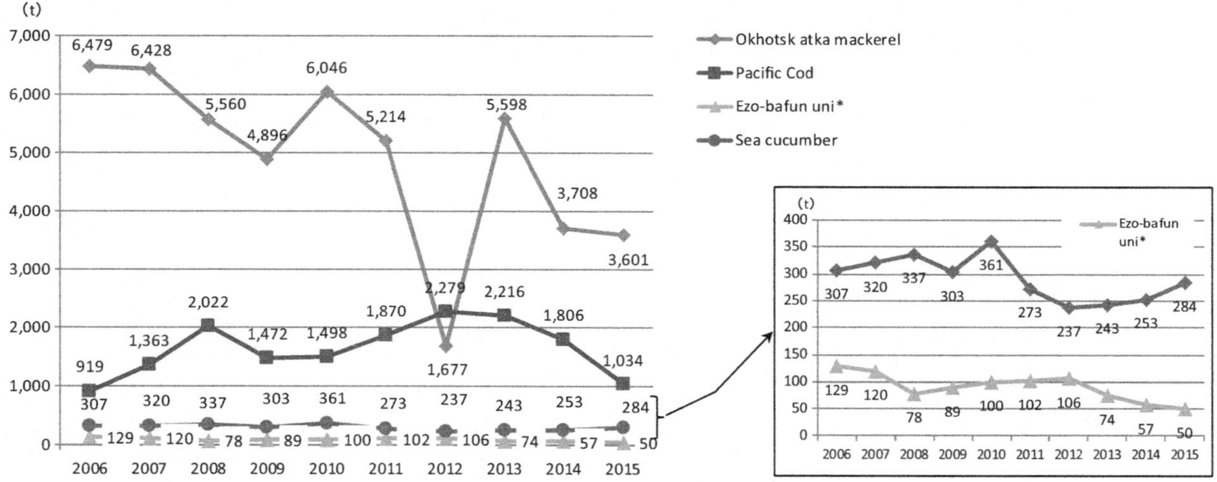

* *Strongylocentrotus intermedius*, a species of sea urchin

Fig. 6.2 Trend in the volume of production for Okhotsk atka mackerel, Pacific cod, and *Ezo-bafun uni** over the last ten years at Rishirifuji-cho, Rishiri-cho, and Rebun-cho. * *Strongylocentrotus intermedius*, a species of sea urchin. Source: These figures were prepared by the author based on data in the below referenced materials: Fisheries Ports Administrator, Rishirifuji Town (2016) "Rishirifuji Fisheries, 2016 Edition" (in Japanese); Community Development Department, Rishiri Town (2016) "Documents Relating to Status of Fisheries Production, 2015" (in Japanese); and Rebun Town (2016) "Trends in Fishery Yields, by Species" (in Japanese)

3 Okhotsk Atka Mackerel and Pacific Cod: Diminishing Catches and Concerns over Depletion of Resources

Catches of Okhotsk atka mackerel and Pacific cod, two of the main species taken by the offshore fishing industry of the islands, have been declining for the past several years (Fig. 6.2). In addition, numbers of northern species of mackerel and cod are low in the waters around both islands, and resources are in decline (Hokkaido, 2016; Hokkaido Government Fisheries Management Section, 2015). As indicated above, a number of causes of this phenomenon can be considered. Nevertheless, recognizing that numbers are low and resources are declining, appropriate resource management based on scientific studies will be essential to maintaining the catch into the future. In part because of the effect of declining production in increasing the unit price of the catch, the total value of production for the islands in the most recent year was higher than the previous year, but like Pacific herring and walleye pollock previously, a drastic decline in resources may make it difficult to maintain a catch at all, leaving the local fishing industry with nothing.

Stocks of northern species of mackerel are particularly low, and for a three-year period from 2012, fisheries operators engaged in voluntary resource management efforts in relation to the fish which saw them reducing their catch volume or their fishing effort by 30%. However, this did not lead to a recovery of mackerel stocks, and the measures were therefore continued for another three years (Hokkaido, 2016). There is no legal restriction on the size of the mackerel catch, and, other than the temporary measures discussed above, the only resource management measures being applied are voluntary restrictions on catch size and fishing period put into effect by each fisheries cooperative association.

In addition, no total allowable catch (TAC) is set for either mackerel or cod under the Act on Preservation and Control of Living Marine Resources. The necessity of adding both species to the list of resources subject to total allowable catch restrictions has been examined at the government level (Expert Panel on the TAC System, Etc., Apr.–Dec., 2008). Ultimately, the species were not added to the list due to a lack of scientific evidence urging the application of TAC restrictions, and a failure to demonstrate that stocks were diminishing (Expert Panel on the TAC System, Etc., 2008). However, as indicated above, stocks of northern species of mackerel and cod did in fact diminish later, and the above-mentioned voluntary resource management measures failed to bear fruit. Concerns have also been raised regarding high-volume trawl net fishing of mackerel by Wakkanai offshore trawling operators in the waters off the islands. To help ensure that there is no repetition of the mistakes made in the cases of Pacific herring and walleye pollock in the waters of the Sea of Japan off Hokkaido, it will be necessary to vigorously promote efforts to develop scientific methods of estimating the volume of fisheries resources and making future projections (both of which are currently difficult), and re-examine the feasibility of regulating catch sizes via effective standards based on TAC restrictions. While accumulating scientific evidence, the Expert Panel on the TAC System, Etc. should conduct ongoing studies concerning the application of TAC restrictions to more species, including the species discussed above, based on the specific characteristics of the resources in question.

4 *Ezo-bafun Uni*: Diminishing Catches and Efforts to Cultivate the Species and Restock Supplies

Catches of *Ezo-bafun uni* have recently displayed a declining tendency (Fig. 6.2). No scientific data concerning the current status of resources is available, and the cause of their decline is also unclear. Local fisheries operators have indicated that *Kita-murasaki uni*, a hardier species inhabiting comparatively deep waters, have begun breeding in the shallows that are the habitat of the *Ezo-bafun uni*, and the latter are disappearing. It has also been suggested that the isolation of the habitats of the two species has been disrupted by factors including increased water temperature and the artificial transplantation of the *Kita-murasaki uni* to the shallows in order to boost their numbers. Whatever the cause, there is concern over the status of sea urchin resources. It would therefore be desirable to see ongoing surveys, including visual surveys, of the volume of sea urchin resources, and efforts to understand sea urchin ecology.

The catch size of sea urchins is regulated by the Regulations for the Management of Hokkaido's Fisheries (Article 35), and in addition the fisheries operators of both islands have voluntarily established even more rigorous restrictions on catch size. In addition, while it is not based on scientific data, the total sea urchin catch for each fisheries cooperative association is recorded in their annual business plans. However, these figures are indicated as being no more than yardsticks.

For many years the Rishiri Town budget (approximately 36 million yen per year) has made funds available for the cultivation of *Ezo-bafun uni* and the restocking of supplies in the waters around the island. Over the course of 21 years, the Rishiri Island Sea Urchin Seed Production Center has produced approximately five million sea urchin seeds per year. Six hundred thousand of these seeds are sold to other organizations (the Rishiri Fisheries Cooperative Association Oshidomari Center and the Wakkanai Fisheries Cooperative Association), and the remainder of the cultivated juvenile sea urchins are released in the waters off the town. Some question the effectiveness of this sea urchin cultivation project in the absence of clear limits on the urchin catch volume. However, a survey conducted in 2008 found that approximately 10% of *Ezo-bafun uni* caught by local fisheries operators had developed from the juveniles released by this project, indicating that outcomes of a specific level are being achieved. In accordance with the government's Basic Principles for Japanese Marine Stock Enhancement, Hokkaido is currently formulating and implementing the 7th Basic Aquaculture Plan (2015–2019), based on Article 6 of the Basic Principles, "Ordinances for the Rehabilitation of Hokkaido's Fishing Industry and Fishing Villages." In addition to establishing the species subject to aquaculture efforts, including *Ezo-bafun uni*, and setting numerical targets for the cultivation of seeds and the release of juveniles, this plan seeks to promote aquaculture suited to the characteristics of the oceans around Hokkaido (the Sea of Japan, the Pacific, and the Sea of Okhotsk) (Hokkaido, 2016). The aquaculture project being conducted in Rishiri Town is one of the main examples of these initiatives. The town is bearing a considerable financial burden, but the initiative is one which will attract attention as a measure to support the future of Rishiri Island's fishing industry.

5 Sea Cucumber: Realization of a Stable Production Volume and Attempts to Expand Production through Seed Cultivation and Release of Juveniles

About ten years ago, the volume of production of sea cucumbers began to increase on both Rishiri and Rebun Islands, and has since become comparatively stable (Fig. 6.2). The majority of these sea cucumbers are exported to China. Hokkaido sea cucumbers are highly prized as a luxury ingredient in Chinese dishes. Demand has increased with the growth of the Chinese economy, and the price of sea cucumbers has risen significantly. Against this background, in Rishiri Town the Rishiri Island Sea Urchin Seed Production Center has commenced a sea cucumber seed cultivation and juvenile release project, and is conducting tests in the island's bays towards increasing the stock of sea cucumbers. In Rishirifuji Town the similar initiative is being conducted in cooperation with the Fisheries Guidance Office. Tests of the cultivation of sea cucumber seeds have also recently been commenced in Rebun Town. These initiatives will support the advancement of the Hokkaido aquaculture industry discussed above. Using its Fisheries Experimental Stations, Hokkaido is currently working to identify the effects of release of the cultivated resources, develop nutritional media to assist in the cultivation of the seeds, and develop low-cost and high-efficiency cultivation techniques (Hokkaido, 2016).

Like for sea urchins, the size of the harvest and the period of harvesting sea cucumbers are regulated by the Regulations for the Management of Hokkaido's Fisheries and the fisheries cooperative associations. However, there are no restrictions on the size of the sea cucumber harvest. Sea cucumber aquaculture is progressing in the islands, but unlike in the case of sea urchins, there does not seem to be concern over unrestricted "Olympic-style" harvesting from the perspective of sustainability. There is certainly room for examination of the pros and cons of introducing some form of control over the volume of the harvest in parallel with the advancement of the aquaculture industry.

6 Conclusion

The fisheries industries of Rishiri and Rebun Islands originated with the modern fishing of Pacific herring. The decline in the herring catch prompted fisheries operators to turn to other species, including Okhotsk atka mackerel and Pacific cod, and these species have been fished up to the present day. Recently, however, the production volumes of these main species, in addition to that of *Ezo-bafun uni*, have been in decline. It is not certain that it will be possible to shift the focus to different species in the future, as it was in the past. Doubts must exist in this respect, given the limited range of species available.

The unit price of the catch will increase if production volumes decline, but the resulting economic benefits to fisheries operators and fisheries cooperative associations in the short term will dampen the incentive to engage in resource management from medium- to long-term perspectives. An increase in the unit price of the catch will also threaten marine product processing businesses, and this will in turn render the goal of transforming the fishing industry into a "sextiary" industry, being pursued by the government in order to halt the industry's decline, a more distant one.[1] The possibility that the decline in fisheries resources will continue, and that the industry will face a crisis in the medium- to long-term, cannot be denied.

It also cannot be denied that with the aging of the fishing population, there is a lack of momentum among the regional community towards the transformation of the fishing industry into one that manages resources with a view to the long-term future. If there were a large number of young fisheries workers, the realization of a fishing industry that would be sustainable far into the future would be a matter of vital importance to the regional community; with few young workers taking up places in the industry, however, the sense of urgency in relation to the future becomes comparatively less strong. In this sense, the realization of appropriate resource management is closely related to the securing and development of young fisheries workers, and the two problems discussed at the outset of this chapter are two sides of the same coin. Given this, the enhancement of fisheries resource management beyond the existing voluntary measures based on objective and scientific data and the realization of a fishing industry that is sustainable from medium- to long-term perspectives would have the potential to work positively in increasing the numbers of young fisheries workers. For regional communities that depend on the fishing industry, this may therefore represent a means of halting depopulation and promoting sustainable development.

The cases of Rishiri Island and Rebun Island give us much to consider. In order to realize sustainable fisheries and regional communities, it will be essential to take a broader perspective in our consideration of legislation and the formulation of policy related to the management of resources, while ensuring that we remain grounded in the actual experiences of the communities themselves.

Acknowledgments The author wishes to express her sincere gratitude to all the individuals concerned at the Center for Research and Promotion of Japanese Islands, the Rishirifuji, Rishiri, and Rebun Town administrations, the Rishiri Island History Museum, the Rishiri Town Museum, the Rebun Town Historical Museum, the Rishiri Fisheries Cooperative Association, the Kafuka Fisheries Cooperative Association, Jinpo Foods (a marine products processing company), the Hokkaido Federation of Fisheries Cooperative Associations, and the Fisheries Section of the

Industry Promotion Department, Soya Regional Development Bureau for their assistance in onsite surveys on Rishiri and Rebun Islands, the provision of relevant data and materials, and the checking of information regarding relevant laws during the writing of this chapter.

This chapter presents part of the outcome of research conducted with the assistance of a Japan Society for the Promotion of Science (JSPS) Grant-in-Aid for Scientific Research and a Mitsubishi Foundation Research Grant in the Humanities (16H03570).

Note

1. The "sextiary" industry, or the "sextiary" sector (sometimes called the "sixth sector,") is a Japanese term referring to the diversification of agriculture into agriculture-related manufacturing and services such as food processing and restaurant management. The concept of a "sixth sector" originates from the idea of combining agricultural production (Primary industry: 1) with processing (Secondary industry: 2) and distribution and sales (Tertiary industry: 3) to generate a synergistic relationship ($1 \times 2 \times 3 = 6$).

References

Community Development Department, Rishiri Town (2016), "*Hesei27nen Gyogyo Seisan Jokyo Shiryo* (Documents Relating to Status of Fisheries Production, 2015)," January, 2016 (In Japanese).

Expert Panel on the TAC System, Etc. (2008), "*TAC-Seido no Kadai to Kaizenhoko (Chukan Torimatome)* (Issues of the TAC System and Directions for Improvements (Interim Report))," September 2008 (In Japanese).

Fisheries Ports Administrator, Rishirifuji Town (2016), "*Hesei28nendoban Rishirifuji-cho no Suisan* (Rishirifuji Fisheries, FY2016 Edition)," April 2016 (In Japanese).

Hokkaido Government, Administration Department, Fisheries and Forestry Division (ed.) (2016), *Hokkaido Suisangyo/Gyoson no Sugata 2016 –Hokkaido Suisan Hakusho* (Hokkaido Fisheries White Paper: State of Hokkaido's Fishing Industry and Fishing Villages, 2016), June 2016, Hokkaido Government (In Japanese).

Hokkaido Government, Fisheries Management Section, Fisheries Bureau, Fisheries and Forestry Division (ed.) (2015), "*Hokkaido Suisanshigen Kanri Manyuaru 2015nendoban* (Manual for Management of Fishery Resources in Hokkaido, FY2015 Edition)," Hokkaido Government, and Fisheries Research Department, Hokkaido Research Organization (In Japanese).

Hokkaido Government, Soya General Subprefectural Bureau, Fisheries Section, Regional Development Department (ed.) (2015), *Soya no Suisan Heisei 25nen-doban* (Soya Fisheries, FY2013 Edition), Hokkaido Government Soya General Subprefectural Bureau, October 2015 (In Japanese).
Rebun Town (2016), "*Gyoshubetsu Gyokakudaka no Suii* (Trends in Fishery Yields, by Species)," February 2016 (In Japanese).

PART III

Regulatory Reforms: Tourism Policy

CHAPTER 7

Tourism Strategy towards 2020: Promotion of Tourism and the Revitalization of Regional Areas

Yasushi Shinohara

Abstract The Japanese government has positioned tourism as part of Japan's regional revitalization strategy and economic growth strategy, and has announced its intention to increase annual numbers of foreign tourists to 30 million. However, the easing of existing tourism-related regulations and change in Japan's readiness to accept foreign tourists, looking towards increasing the depth of tourism in the nation, will be essential for a tourism strategy which seeks to compete with other countries around the world. This chapter provides an overview of relevant issues and presents a number of proposals. This chapter also introduces the next two chapters by two experts examining the concept of Japanese-style destination marketing organizations (DMOs) and the issue of *minpaku*, paid accommodations using private houses or apartments, to provide suggestions for concrete policy orientations in both areas.

Keywords Tourism strategy • Regional revitalization • Regulatory reform • Inbound tourism • Japanese tourists • Destination-based tourism • Destination marketing organization (DMO)

Y. Shinohara (✉)
The Faculty of Tourism and Community Studies,
Atomi University, Tokyo, Japan

T. Hatta (ed.), *Economic Challenges Facing Japan's Regional Areas*,
https://doi.org/10.1007/978-981-10-7110-2_7

1 Introduction

In 2013, the Japanese government realized its much-desired goal of achieving a figure of ten million foreign visitors to Japan (inbound tourists). In FY 2016, 24.04 million visitors were recorded, and the 20 million mark was broken. The total amount of spending in Japan by foreign tourists also increased in 2016, to 3.7476 trillion yen, the highest-ever figure. And it was in 2015 when the first sharp increase in the amount of spending by foreign tourists was observed, to 3.4771 trillion yen, and that was the first time the amount had exceeded three trillion yen in a year. This represented a 71.5% increase against the figure of 2.278 trillion yen for the previous year. Positioning tourism as part of its strategy for regional revitalization and economic growth, the government has now announced a new goal, raising its target for the annual number of foreign visitors to Japan to 40 million (Ministry of Land, Infrastructure, Transportation and Tourism, 2015; The Prime Minister of Japan and His Cabinet, 2016). However, the easing of existing tourism-related regulations and innovation in Japan's readiness to accept foreign tourists, looking towards increasing the depth of tourism in the nation, will be essential for a tourism strategy which seeks to compete with other countries around the world. This chapter provides an overview of relevant issues and presents a number of proposals. For the following two chapters in this section, we asked experts on the concept of Japanese-style destination marketing organizations (DMOs), which will offer a foundation to boost regional revitalization and tourism in Japan to a new level, and on the issue of ***minpaku***, which is attracting controversy in relation to the easing of accommodation regulations against the background of a chronic shortage of hotel accommodation in Japan's large metropolitan areas, to provide us with suggestions for concrete policy orientations in both areas (Fig. 7.1).

2 Tourism in Japan: Status and Issues

According to international balance of payments statistics for Japan, the travel balance recorded a surplus in FY 2014 for the first time in 55 years. The rapid increase in foreign visitors to Japan became a talking point, but what we should focus on here is the decline in the amount of domestic travel expenditure by Japanese tourists. The figure declined by around two trillion yen in 2014. A major factor in this decline was a rapid shift in the type of travel undertaken by Japanese tourists, from the traditional

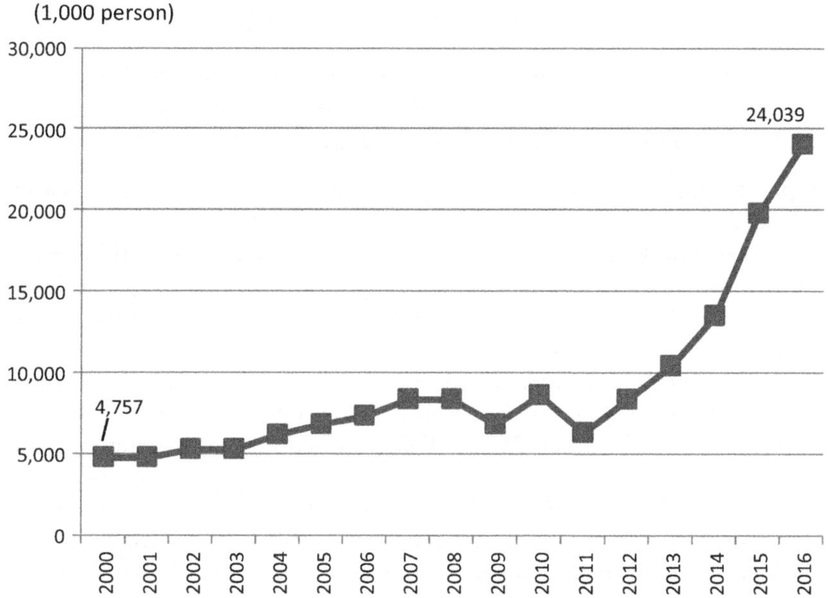

Fig. 7.1 Changes in the number of foreign tourists visiting Japan. Source: Japan Tourism Agency, White Paper on Tourism, each year. Original source was documents compiled by the MLIT (Ministry of Land, Infrastructure, Transport and Tourism) based on documents by the Ministry of Justice (2000–2008), and estimation by Japan National Tourism Organization (2009–2016)

group tour type, in which tourists travel to a variety of destinations, to individual travel focused on experience, which tends to see the traveler staying at a specific destination. Innovation in domestic tourism products in response to this change is severely delayed. The tourism industry in Japan grew with a central focus on domestic demand, and now faces a major turning point. It must turn away from a model in which tourist areas have been developed and tourists catered for based on traditional group-oriented tourism, towards the restructuring of Japanese tourism in its entirety, while also bringing overseas tourists into its purview. The issue here will be to promote the easing of tourism-related regulations and boost the floating population of Japan's regions with the tourism industry as the central axis. I believe this will function as a driving force for regional revitalization.

3 Issues towards 2020

3.1 Creation of Japanese-style Destination Marketing/Management Organizations (DMOs) as a Foundation to Boost Regional Revitalization and Tourism to a New Level

Rapid population decline in Japan's rural areas is resulting in increasing contraction of regional economies (Kaneko, 2016; Masuda, 2015). Against this background, increasing the vitality of regional areas by boosting the non-resident population, that is, promoting regional development by increasing tourism, is an important policy issue in relation to regional revitalization. Attention is being focused here on the launch of Japanese versions of DMOs, tourist organizations which are standard features of advanced tourist regions such as Europe and the USA (The Prime Minister of Japan and His Cabinet, 2016). This issue is discussed in detail in Chap. 8, "Creation of DMOs to Promote Inbound Tourism: Methods and Issues," by Professor Yoshitaka Mizoo (2018). The concept for the Japanese-style DMOs being advocated by the government is "independently-operated organizations established with the aim of marketing and promoting (branding) tourist areas (regional tourism resources), possessing functions for management of the quality (safety) of services for the acceptance of tourists, the formulation of tourism strategies, and the management of business planning," which work to assist in regional revitalization.[1] One major issue is promoting a higher proportion of visits to regional areas by foreign tourists. The functioning of these DMOs in regional tourist areas and their ability to newly create environments that allow for the acceptance of foreign tourists, and to put in place measures for the cultivation of the necessary human resources and to functionally implement them in regional areas, represent two major factors in successfully increasing visits to regional areas by overseas tourists.

3.2 New Directions in Accommodation Facilities in Japan: Discussion Is Increasing around the Minpaku *Issue*

To recap issues discussed in detail by Professor Kumiko Tomikawa in Chap. 9, "Towards the Relaxation of Regulations on *Minpaku* in Japan," (Tomikawa, 2018) there is a chronic shortage of hotel spaces in large metropolitan areas in Japan, in particular Tokyo and Osaka. This is considered to be due to the doubling of the number of overseas tourists visiting Japan in the two-year period from 2013. In Tokyo, where a 75% hotel occupancy rate was previously considered good, occupancy rates are in excess of 90%, and there is an ongoing inability to ensure accommodation for business travelers. Looking towards 2020, an even greater shortfall in accommodation facilities is looming, but spiraling construction costs mean that it will be difficult to ensure a sufficient number of rooms to respond to the expected demand. Overseas, there is an active sharing economy. The website Airbnb, which connects people seeking to rent accommodation with people needing accommodation, already covers more than 800,000 rooms and other accommodations located in 33,000 cities in 192 countries (Ozawa and Machida, 2015).

However, because rental contracts of less than 30 days' duration are subject to restrictions based on the Hotel Business Act, and because it is not possible to offer short-term rentals without satisfying the conditions required for accommodation facilities, for example having a reception desk, the use of this sharing economy is not allowed in Japan.

In order to break through this particular "bedrock regulation," the government is allowing the offering of accommodation for less than 30 days by private individuals or businesses which are not registered as hotels, termed *minpaku* in Japanese, in special zones in which the restrictions of the Hotel Business Act in this respect do not apply. As pioneering examples of these strategic *minpaku* zones, Tokyo's Ota Ward and Osaka City have formulated independent regulations, and independent *minpaku* businesses commenced legal operation from 2016. The regulations provide measures for the prevention of illegal residence for purposes of crime or terrorism, and to respond to complaints from neighbors regarding noise or garbage. At the same time, new measures for the revitalization of the special zones through their existing economic activities are being put into effect, with the administrations involved in the establishment of the special zones using the formulation of the new regulations as an opportunity to promote increased circulation in their local economies by attempting to increase the appeal of their areas to *minpaku* users through initiatives such as offering free tickets for the use of local public baths, and to boost tourist spending at local stores and restaurants by issuing coupons that can be exchanged for various services and printing maps in a variety of languages.

In addition, as Professor Tomikawa indicates in her chapter, in its attempt to increase the annual number of overseas visitors to Japan to 40 million, the government has also established a policy of treating *minpaku* businesses as "budget hotels" under the Hotel Business Act as a second move in its easing of the regulations on *minpaku*, and is reviewing the possibility of expanding legal recognition of *minpaku* nationwide, but it is feared that this step would face serious opposition from existing *ryokan* owners.

4 Conclusion

This chapter has considered issues facing Japan's tourism strategy as it looks towards 2020 and the easing of tourism-related regulations for the promotion of regional revitalization. However, while the goal of making Japan a tourism-oriented nation and realizing a significant increase in the annual number of overseas visitors from a base of 20 million in 2016 to 40 million by 2020 is an important one, we must be careful not to merely prioritize the achievement of the target figures. It would be desirable to see comprehensive discussion of the positioning of the tourism industry in Japan covering aims such as what type of people from which countries we seek to attract, for which purposes, and whether we seek to encourage single or repeat visits; these discussions should also encompass concrete measures for the revitalization of tourism demand among the Japanese themselves. We must promote the development of tourism as a new engine of regional revitalization and growth in the Japanese economy which will become a major pillar of economic reform.

Acknowlegements I should like to express my deepest appreciation to Professor Hiroyuki Yasujima of Atomi University for his great help and generous support in pushing forward this study.

Note

1. An excerpt from Japan Travel and Tourism Association (2015), "*Nihonban DMO no Tebiki* (Outline of Japanese-style DMO)" (www.mlit.go.jp/common/001110766.pdf) (in Japanese).

References

Kaneko, Isamu (2016), *Chiho-sosei to shometsu no Shakaigaku* (Sociology on Regional Revitalization and Disappearance), Minerva Shobo (in Japanese).

Masuda, Hiroya (2015), *Tokyo Shometsu: Kaigohatan to chiho-ijuh* (Disappearing Tokyo: Nursing Care Bankruptcy and Emigration to the Local Regions), Chuko Shinsho (in Japanese).

Ministry of Land, Infrastructure, Transport and Tourism (2015), '*Kanko wo meguru genjo to kadai toh ni tsuite* (Current Status and Issues of Tourism in Japan),' Document submitted by Keiichi Ishii, Minister of Land, Infrastructure, Transport and Tourism, for the first meeting of '*Asuno Nihon wo sasaeru kanko bijon kohsohkaigi* (Committee for designing visions for tourism to support future Japan),' November 9, 2015 (in Japanese).

Mizoo, Yoshitaka (2018), "Creation of DMOs to Promote Inbound Tourism: Methods and Issues," in T. Hatta (ed.), *Economic Challenges Facing Japan's Regional Areas*, Plagrave Macmillan, pp. 75–82.

Ozawa, Wataru and Machida, Ryuma (2015), *Chuko apahto / manshon ga umarekawaru: Airbnb Akishitsubukken katsuyojutsu* (Regenerating used appartments/condominiums: Utilization of vacancy properties by Airbnb), Gentosha Media Consulting (in Japanese).

The Prime Minister of Japan and His Cabinet (2016), "*Asuno Nihon wo sasaeru kanko bijon* (Visions for tourism to support future Japan)," March 30, 2016 (in Japanese).

Tomikawa, Kumiko (2018), "Towards the Relaxation of Regulations on *Minpaku* in Japan," in T. Hatta (ed.), *Economic Challenges Facing Japan's Regional Areas*, Plagrave Macmillan, pp. 83–89.

CHAPTER 8

Creation of DMOs to Promote Inbound Tourism: Methods and Issues

Yoshitaka Mizoo

Abstract The trend towards the use of inbound tourism to drive regional revitalization is increasing in strength in Japan. Enabling the nation's regions to attract tourists is therefore an urgent task. Destination marketing/management organizations (DMOs) are one response. Their roles would include providing information, conducting promotions, implementing effective marketing, and formulating strategies.

Regional areas attempting to create DMOs would be required to evaluate the resources they possess and decide on their travel products. It would then be essential to create a strategy regarding where and how to sell these products. Furthermore, it would be necessary to strengthen tourism associations. Cooperation between tourism associations and various regional bodies, including commerce and industry associations, would be vitally important factors.

Keywords Destination Marketing/Management Organization (DMO) • Tourism association • Tourism resources • Travel product • Community tourism • Destination-based tourism • Sextiary sector

Y. Mizoo (✉)
Rikkyo University, Saitama, Japan

T. Hatta (ed.), *Economic Challenges Facing Japan's Regional Areas*,
https://doi.org/10.1007/978-981-10-7110-2_8

1 Introduction

In Japan, the trend towards the use of inbound tourism to drive regional revitalization is increasing in strength. Against the background of an increasing number of overseas visitors to Japan, ensuring that the nation's regions are ready to accept tourists is an urgent task. DMOs are one response. DMO is short for destination marketing/management organization. These are tourism promotion organizations established under the auspices of regional areas themselves. Their roles include providing information, conducting promotions, implementing effective marketing, and formulating strategy.

This chapter discusses effective means of evaluating regional resources when regional areas begin to create DMOs and indicates a number of approaches in relation to DMO strategies which should be adopted by regional areas.

Prior to commencing this discussion, the following two points should be made: First, in relation to regional areas (here referring to the regional city, town, or village level), "inbound tourism" refers not only to tourism involving overseas visitors to Japan, but to all visitors from outside the specific region, including Japanese citizens; foreign tourists represent a subset of tourists from outside the region. Second, while "Japanese-style DMOs" are now being hurriedly created under the leadership of the Japan Tourism Agency, they already have precedents in the USA and Europe. It is this type of DMO that Japan should be striving to create. "DMO" here therefore refers to "universal DMO" rather than "specifically Japanese DMO."

The success or failure of a DMO depends on whether or not the regional area creating it is able to express its individual character in its initiatives. This chapter suggests a framework for DMO strategy, and it is the author's hope that individual regions will deploy their own regionally specific DMOs based on this framework.

2 Evaluation of Tourism Resources Possessed by Regional Areas—the Target Market is the Determinant

Tourism can be viewed in a narrow sense, as concerned with "sightseeing" for the purpose of "looking" and "learning," or in a broader sense, encompassing "recreation" and "accommodation." Regional areas attempting to create DMOs must evaluate the resources they possess and determine whether, as a travel destination, they are one or other of these, or whether they have the characteristics of both. It is also essential for regions to decide on their travel products after learning as much as possible about which areas they are able to attract visitors from and what the preferences and behavioral characteristics of people from those areas are (Mizoo 2015).

2.1 *Is the Area a "Sightseeing Area"?*

The type associated with tourism in the narrow sense, as "sightseeing," is basically the tour, on which tourists visit a number of places in a specific area.

In order to attract tourists to a region, it is essential first to understand the characteristics of the resources that the region possesses as a sightseeing area. "Characteristics" here refers to the types of resources and the appeal of the individual resources. Based on the types of resources possessed by the region, it can be decided what individual themes tourism products can be created around. Regional knowledge will be applied to determining themes that will attract visitors to particular places—culture, history, flowers, and so forth.

In addition, the regions from which visitors can be attracted (from overseas, throughout Japan, regionally, within the prefecture, or from neighboring prefectures) will be decided based on whether the appeal possessed by individual resources is high or low. At present, there is no method of evaluating the level of appeal of resources other than comparing them with existing sightseeing resources within Japan (Japan Travel Bureau Foundation, 2014).[1] If the resources possess a strong appeal, it will be possible for the region to attract visitors from more remote areas. What must be borne in mind is that the further the distance to be traveled from the point of departure to the destination, the more time and expense is involved in the travel, meaning generally that more days are involved in the trip, and the trip covers a wider area. Because of this, for tourists from distant locations, the program of travel offered must not be restricted to a single region or prefecture. This point is illustrated by the distances traveled over the seven Japan Tourism Agency-designated wide-area sightseeing routes (spanning different prefectures) targeting foreign tourists, such as the Dragon Route.[2]

By contrast, if the appeal of the regional resources is low, or the level of appeal changes with the seasons (flowers, events, annual festivals, etc.), one specific area will be the focus, and in such cases it would be desirable to provide information in a timely fashion to nearby markets.

The author has past experience in presenting Tokyo tourist products and regional attractions separately to overseas markets, the national Japanese market, and the market comprised by regions close to Tokyo and the broader Kanto region. This would presumably be an effective approach at the prefectural level.

2.2 *Is the Area a "Recreation Area"?*

This section looks at "recreation areas," with recreation considered an aspect of tourism in the broader sense. Taking golf and skiing as representative examples, the characteristic of recreational tourism is to stay in the chosen destination and spend time performing the desired activity. Rather than moving between a number of locations, this type of tourism involves a simple round trip between the point of departure and the destination, and a short traveling time is therefore desirable. Because Japan possesses numerous recreation destinations with a high degree of interchangeability, recreation areas make nearby heavily populated markets their main targets. A perfect example of this is the high volume of tourists traveling to Japan from Korea in order to play golf or ski. The fact that large numbers of tourists come to Japan from Australia to ski is due to the availability of good-quality powder snow in Japan during the off season in Australia, which attracts Australian skiers during the Japan ski season. Because the trip from Australia involves time and expense, in this case the amount of time that these tourists spend in Japan is longer (Mizoo 2009).

2.3 *Is the Area an "Accommodation Area"?*

Depending on the conditions of the location, there are three types of "accommodation area" (another aspect of tourism in the broader sense), as follows:

1) the area is a sightseeing area, is on a sightseeing route, or there is a sightseeing area nearby;
2) the area doubles as an accommodation area because it is a recreation area in which tourists choose to stay;
3) in areas which are solely accommodation areas, visitors come from nearby regions.

In terms of the resources of accommodation areas, if we consider Japanese tourists specifically, the presence of a hot spring is a major attraction. Other than this, areas of scenic beauty and areas with beautiful natural environments are selected as accommodation areas. As the distance that visitors have to travel to reach the area becomes higher, the quality and scale of accommodation facilities becomes an issue (both individually and in the region as a whole). At the same time, as the recent popularity of guesthouses indicates, there are travelers who are prepared to stay for longer periods in simple accommodation if the cost is kept down.

2.4 Diversity of Preferences of Overseas Tourists

With regard to foreign visitors to Japan, there are differences between the interests of Westerners and Asians, and among Westerners themselves, of people from, for example, the USA, France, and Germany, and they will naturally choose different destinations and activities in Japan. In the case of Muslim tourists in particular, if there is insufficient awareness of culinary and religious requirements, it will not be possible to meet the needs of guests. Ultimately, it is essential to have a strategy for the provision of information to target markets, and for the acceptance of visitors from those markets. It must also be borne in mind that as they come to visit Japan more often, the destinations, desired activities, and preferences even of people from the same country will change.

3 Establishing Strong DMOs

3.1 Communication of Information from the Region

Next, once a product has been created, it is essential to have a strategy for where and how to sell the product. This generally means selling the product to a travel company, but it is difficult to rely entirely on travel companies, because their focus is normally the entire country, and they tend to disregard regions and tourism resources which have a low level of recognition. However, because even travel companies do not possess a comprehensive knowledge of new themes and tourism resources, it is important for the destination region to continue to actively provide information, prompting awareness and promoting the commercialization of travel products in the target regions. Today, of course, business-to-customer

(B2C) activity is a major focus in addition to business-to-business (B2B) custom, and in this era of social networking services (SNS), it will be necessary for destination regions to continuously provide fresh information to interested parties via computer and other information devices.

The appropriate originator of this information will differ depending on the target market. For nearby markets, it will be sufficient for small regional cities, towns, or villages to provide tourist information. If the entire nation is the target market, then the initiative will shift to the prefectural level. In the case of overseas markets, cooperation will transcend the prefectural level—for example, all prefectures in Kyushu would collaborate to sell to foreign markets. In fact, the names of prefectures or city wards are not recognized in overseas markets. We should consider this from the tourist's perspective. For tourists, the names Yokohama, Kamakura, and Hakone have greater recognition than Kanagawa Prefecture; the names Asakusa and Ueno are more recognizable than Taito Ward. These are the names that we should lead with. The level at which it is possible to do this is that of the provision of information.

This represents what I will term region-led destination-based tourism.

3.2 *Intra-regional Cooperation—the Advancement of Community Tourism*

There are in fact few examples of successful destination-based tourism. In order to make it a reality, it will be essential to strengthen traditional tourism associations, and to do away with a model of reliance on the government or regional administration. We need to cultivate for-profit businesses, and deploy specialist staff. Cooperation between enhanced tourism associations and various regional bodies, including chambers of commerce, agricultural cooperatives, and fisheries cooperatives, and, above all else, a warmly welcoming populace, will be vitally important factors.

The movement towards turning tourism associations into incorporated associations is a first step towards strengthening the organizations, but nevertheless many remain dependent on the government. Against this background, in 2003 the Niseko Resort Tourist Association became the first tourist association in Japan to become an incorporated company.[3] In addition to independently registering travel businesses and conducting a variety of profit-making businesses, the Niseko Resort Tourist Association has commenced community FM broadcasts and also commissions the operation of roadside tourist centers. We can point to the Nagasaki Prefecture Convention and Tourism Association as an example at the prefectural level.

This incorporated foundation is almost entirely independent from the government, and is able, depending on circumstances, to ally itself with special travel businesses in a way that would be difficult for government organizations. The Association's number of employees and budget scale is far and away greater than those of other prefectures. The Tokyo Convention & Visitors Bureau, a public interest incorporated foundation, has added a new function for the organization of conventions to the traditional tourist association, enabling it to mount multifaceted initiatives. Other than these organizational considerations, the willingness of the government, tourist associations, and chambers of commerce to engage in dialogue when needed, as in the cases of Yonezawa, Kusatsu, and Yufuin-Onsen, will also be an important factor.

As exemplified by eco-tourism, "community (-based) tourism," which is being promoted in developing nations, creates a system of intra-regional economic circulation in which tourists are attracted to a specific region, and the majority of their expenditure occurs within the region. Local guides show tourists the region's tourism resources, tourists eat at restaurants that serve local cuisine, they purchase souvenirs at shops selling products made by local people, they stay in locally funded accommodation facilities, and so on.

Even if destination-based tourism does not present a similarly complete system, for the sake of cooperation between local residents and related organizations, it is important to recognize that it is the supply of raw materials and products from the region's primary and secondary industries and from other tertiary industries that supports the tourist industry. When the close relationship between these industries and the tourist industry is made clear, it is possible for people to see that the economic effects of tourism extend broadly throughout the region. Increasing the economic success of the tourist industry has a positive effect on other industries. Today, we are seeing primary industry itself striving to become a "sextiary sector,"[4] and secondary industries are organizing factory visits and selling products directly to tourists. By connecting these primary and secondary industries directly with tourists (consumers), it is possible to see clearly the direction for strong-selling products, creating new economic effects.

The significance of tourism for Japan's regions, and the purpose of working to promote tourism, is understood in initiatives of this type. However, the purpose of tourism is not merely to produce economic benefits, but also, by welcoming people from outside the region, including foreign tourists, to promote their understanding of a culture which was initially strange to them, and to realize personal growth in the people of the region by means of the mutual stimulation occurring through exchange with visitors to the region.

If tourists like the places that they visit, various areas in the region will soon become well known, increasing that region's brand power. If the region's recognition increases, then it will become easier for its primary and secondary industries to find markets if they choose to sell their products outside the region. And if the people of the region are told how desirable their home region is when they visit other parts of the country, they will develop pride in their region. A town that is desirable to live in will be a town that is desirable to visit. The type of organization able to make this a reality is precisely the type of DMO that Japan's regions should be attempting to create.

Notes

1. For methods of evaluation of the level of appeal of tourist resources, see *Utsukushiki Nihon: Tabi no Fuko*, published by the Japan Travel Bureau Foundation.
2. The Dragon Route is a project in which nine prefectures in the Chubu and Hokuriku regions (Aichi, Gifu, Mie, Shizuoka, Nagano, Ishikawa, Toyama, Fukui, and Shiga) have joined together to attract overseas tourists.
3. The majority of conventional tourist associations at the prefectural level are incorporated associations or incorporated foundations, while the majority at the town and village level are voluntary organizations.
4. The "sextiary" industry, or the "sextiary sector" (sometimes called the "sixth sector"), is a Japanese term referring to the diversification of agriculture into agriculture-related manufacturing and services such as food processing and restaurant management. The concept of a "sixth sector" originates from the idea of combining agricultural production (Primary industry: 1) with processing (Secondary industry: 2) and distribution and sales (Tertiary industry: 3) to generate a synergistic relationship ($1 \times 2 \times 3 = 6$).

References

Japan Travel Bureau Foundation (2014), "Utsukushi Nihon (Excellent Japan—A Scenic Portfolio)," JTB Publishing (In Japanese).

Mizoo, Yoshitaka (ed.) (2009), *Kanko-gaku no kiso* (Basics of Tourism),"Hara Shobo (in Japanese).

Mizoo, Yoshitaka (2015), "*Kaitei-ban Kanko-gaku: Kiso to jissen* (Tourism: Basics and Practices (revised edition))," Kokon Shoin (in Japanese).

CHAPTER 9

Towards the Relaxation of Regulations on *Minpaku* in Japan

Kumiko Tomikawa

Abstract A proliferation of Internet *minpaku* sites, leading to a conspicuous increase in the number of users in Japan, has focused attention on the issue of *minpaku*, because the conditions of this type of renting may violate Japan's Hotel Business Act. Discussion of the relaxation of regulations on *minpaku* has proceeded in response to a shortage of hotel rooms and the need to attract overseas visitors. The relaxation of regulations on farm stays in Japan and short-term accommodation in the USA and Europe can serve as references for the relaxation of regulations. Two additional points must be considered in future initiatives towards the relaxation of regulations on *minpaku* in Japan: the formulation of independent bylaws in regional areas, and the promotion of internal tourism.

Keywords *Minpaku* • Regulations • Relaxation • Tourism

K. Tomikawa (✉)
The Faculty of Commercial Sciences, Hiroshima Shudo University, Hiroshima, Japan

T. Hatta (ed.), *Economic Challenges Facing Japan's Regional Areas*,
https://doi.org/10.1007/978-981-10-7110-2_9

1 The Hotel Business Act and *Minpaku*

"*Minpaku*" is the Japanese term for providing rooms in private houses as accommodation. In itself, *minpaku* is not illegal. However, *minpaku* conditions which may violate Japan's Hotel Business Act are today coming under scrutiny. A period of 30 days represents a yardstick for the Hotel Business Act and the Act on Land and Building Leases: If offering a rental contract of under 30 days' duration, it is necessary to seek approval from the prefectural governor to operate as a hotel business.

The Hotel Business Act defines four categories of hotel business: hotels, *ryokan* (Japanese-style inns), budget hotels, and boarding or lodging houses. *Minshuku* (guesthouses or bed and breakfasts) and weekly apartments are normally classified in the budget hotel business category, for which there are no regulations concerning the minimum number of rooms or the minimum length of stay. In order to receive approval to operate a business in this category, each room must be at least 33 cubic meters, and strict safety and other standards must be satisfied (for example, there must be a reception desk, the walls must be made of flame-retardant materials, and smoke detectors must be installed). Because of this, a significant outlay in investment for facilities and equipment would be necessary for an ordinary house to receive approval as a business of this type. Generally, establishments which receive approval to be operated as businesses are classified as *minshuku*, and those which do not are classified as *minpaku*. The stipulations of the Hotel Business Act and the Act on Land and Building Leases are, however, out of step with the present era, and it is time for reconsideration of the acts.

2 The Spread of *Minpaku* and Regulation

The subject of *minpaku* is regularly taken up in the mass media, and there is broad awareness of the issue, but this has only been the case in the middle of 2015. Prior to this, the term *minpaku* would have been understood by most people as referring to boarding in a home in the country while engaging in work on a farm or in the fisheries. This "farm *minpaku*" was advanced as a means of promoting tourism in Japan's regional areas. From spring 2015, however, *minpaku* sites began to proliferate on the Internet, and there was a conspicuous increase in the number of *minpaku* users. With the tragic death as the result of an accidental fall of a young Chinese woman staying in a *minpaku* in Tokyo in July 2015, the issue rapidly came to the public's attention. Surveying Airbnb, the largest service for the introduction of *minpaku* accommodation to potential customers, in order to gauge expansion of the *minpaku* phenomenon, we find that there were 21,000 properties registered in Japan in the year of 2015 (an increase of 374% against the previous year), and the number of users reached one million (an increase of 530% against the previous year).[1] *Minpaku* takes a variety of forms, including homestays, in which the user stays in the landlord's house, and a type in which the user rents an apartment or house. For tourists, the homestay type offers a unique experience, involving exchanges with locals and cultural experiences; the rental type makes it easy for a family or group to stay multiple nights. This latter type is particularly common in Japan. It is thought that because there are a limited number of extended-stay facilities or facilities enabling users to cook for themselves in Japan, there is a demand for this rental type, and that for the renters it represents an effective use of empty space, while for users renting their own space is a comfortable option in a culture in which shared rooms and shared houses are not the norm. Some people fear, however, that this rental type, as opposed to the homestay type, will result in issues such as noise and the violation of community rules, and even create the conditions for crime.

In the USA and Europe, people have traditionally stayed with relatives and acquaintances while traveling, but from around the mid-2000s, the number of sites offering short-term accommodation in private houses began to increase, and sites enabling direct reservations to be made appeared. This highlighted a variety of issues, including legal problems. Against this background, Airbnb spread rapidly following its foundation in the USA in 2008, and new bylaws began to be enacted as a result in numerous US and European cities. As this indicates, unlike in Japan, the issue of *minpaku*, and responses to it, are already well established in the USA and Europe.

Given this history, the relaxation of regulations on farm lodgings in Japan and short-term accommodation in private residences in the USA and Europe can serve as references in relation to the relaxation of regulations on *minpaku* in Japan.

Efforts to promote *minpaku* in farming communities commenced in the town of Ajimu in Oita Prefecture, which has welcomed large numbers of domestic and overseas tourists since it commenced its initiative in 1996. Because Ajimu offers *minpaku* with meals, as the number of tourists increased, concerns that the enterprise might violate the Hotel Business

Act and the Food Sanitation Act were raised. At the time, the Ministry of Agriculture, Forestry and Fisheries was promoting green tourism (involving city people engaging in leisure activities while staying in farming or fishing villages) as a policy, and encouraged the registration of *minshuku* enabling guests to experience agricultural and fisheries work to form the core of this effort. However, the barriers to normal houses in fishing or farming villages being granted approval to operate as *minshuku* were high, and the law impeded the entry of new operators to the market. The authorities ultimately took the experience of Ajimu and the problems of registering *minshuku* into consideration, and from 2002 relaxed regulations such as standards for minimum floor area in order to promote green tourism. It is interesting to note that *minshuku* in Ajimu are termed either *nohaku* (farm stays) or *minpaku*, and some continue to be termed *minpaku* even when they receive approval to operate as businesses under the Hotel Business Act.

Turning to the situation in the USA and Europe, I would like to look in particular at regulations concerning landlords seeking to offer *minpaku* services. In Rome, *minpaku* is not allowed, and anyone wishing to accept short-term guests must register as a hotel, but most municipalities in the USA and Europe offer approval for *minpaku* when they are notified. In the case of Berlin, however, while the city has a system for granting approval for *minpaku*, it is prohibited in many of the city's districts, and numerous actions violate city laws and ordinances. In New York, renting space in an apartment building for a period of less than 30 days is prohibited. In other cities around the world, approval is not required but other conditions apply: In London, landlords can rent space for no more than 90 days per year; in Amsterdam the figure is 60 days, and a maximum of four people are allowed at any one time; in Paris, the landlord must reside in the residence for at least eight months of the year. In addition to regulations of this type, many cities demand the payment of taxes including tourism tax, short-term accommodation tax, and income tax.

As the discussion above has shown, in Japan regulations on *minpaku* have been relaxed in specific areas and for specific types of enterprise. In the USA and Europe, attempts are being made to limit encroachment on residential areas and communities and to mitigate the effect on existing short-term accommodation facilities by establishing conditions in specific municipalities and districts to restrict length of stay and the scale of short-term renting. These examples are receiving attention in current discussions on the relaxation of regulations on *minpaku*.

3 Discussion on the Relaxation of Regulations

The Japanese government is proceeding with the relaxation of regulations on *minpaku* in specific areas, and in October 2015 allowed the provision of accommodation for periods of up to 30 days on the basis of a rental contract as an exception to the Hotel Business Act. Giving consideration to the operation of hotels and *ryokan*, the exception to the Act stipulates that in principle the rooms should be offered to foreign visitors to Japan for no less than seven days, and include special conditions regarding, for example, the prevention of nuisance to neighbors. Given that the majority of foreign tourists stay no more than six days in Japan, the feasibility of the provision has been called into question, but Tokyo's Ota Ward and Osaka City, both of which are experiencing a serious shortage of hotel accommodation, have enacted bylaws allowing *minpaku*. Separately to initiatives in these special zones, the Ministry of Health, Labour and Welfare and the Ministry of Land, Infrastructure, Transport and Tourism established the Investigative Commission regarding the Orientation for *Minpaku* Services in November 2015. The Investigative Commission met 13 times, and published its final report on June 20, 2016. During its period of deliberation, the Investigative Commission established guidelines that position *minpaku* accommodation as "budget hotels" under the Hotel Business Act, and relaxed regulations including the standard for floor area in order to make it easier for landlords to receive approval (effective as of April 1, 2017).[2] Based on the final report of the Investigative Commission, it is expected that regulations concerning intermediary businesses will be revised in the future, and revision of the Hotel Business Act will also proceed. Therefore, both the administrations of the special zones and the Investigative Commission regarding the Orientation for *Minpaku* Services are basically aiming towards the promotion of *minpaku* by means of the relaxation of regulations. The contradiction in the fact that the former recognize *minpaku* as an exception to the Hotel Business Act, while the latter situates it within the compass of the Act, has been noted. The contradiction exists because the administrations of the special zones view *minpaku* on the basis of the Act on Land and Building Leases, and the current policy direction can be seen as a compromise between this Act and the Hotel Business Act. Whatever the case, the two approaches have entirely different scopes of application, with the former focused on special areas, and the latter taking in the entire country.

4 Towards Future Initiatives

Discussion of the relaxation of regulations on *minpaku* has proceeded on the basis of Japan's worsening shortage of hotel rooms and with the measures being seen as part of efforts to attract a greater number of overseas visitors. However, if we look at the occupancy rate of rooms throughout the country (in October 2015), we find a rate of around 80% for hotels, around 40% for *ryokan*, and less than 30% for budget hotels. The occupancy rate for *ryokan* and budget hotels is around 60% in Tokyo, and only about 50% in Osaka. In addition, foreign visitors represent only around 10% of users of short-term accommodation throughout the country, and in Tokyo, 70% of users are visiting for purposes other than sightseeing.[3] In other words, the shortage of hotel rooms is mainly restricted to the Osaka metropolitan area, and is especially serious for business travelers; however, rooms remain to be filled in small-scale facilities, and the occupancy of facilities in rural areas is in a slump. Given this, promotion of the use of regional accommodation facilities by groups, which are unable to stay in large cities, would represent an opportunity for the realization of regional revitalization.

Two points must be considered in future initiatives towards the relaxation of regulations on *minpaku*. One of these is the formulation of independent bylaws in regional areas. The circumstances surrounding *minpaku* differ in different regions. In the special zones designated by the government, there are serious shortages of hotel accommodation; in hot spring areas, in which supervision of illegal *minpaku* is being enhanced, there are numerous *ryokan*, but the number of visitors has slumped. It is important that even as the government sets out a direction for *minpaku*, municipalities and local administrations do not simply wait passively for the government's guidelines, but formulate their own independent guidelines to enable them to use *minpaku* in the revitalization of their regions. Removing restrictions on *minpaku* may be an effective means of promoting the invigoration of tourism in Japan, but the strategy of relying on the rapidly changing inbound market in order to boost tourism is a dangerous one. Japan will not become the tourism-oriented nation it seeks to become unless it works to promote both inbound and internal tourism. The realization of more widespread *minpaku* would be desirable from the perspectives of both promoting internal tourism and contributing to regional revitalization.

Notes

1. Airbnb (https://www.airbnb.jp/about/about-us) January 25, 2016 (in Japanese).
2. Japan Tourism Agency, '*Minpaku sabisu no arikata ni kansuru kentoh-kai saishuhoukokusho* (Advisory council on *Minpaku* service),' final report (in Japanese) September 09, 2016 (http://www.mlit.go.jp/common/001135805.pdf).
3. Japan Tourism Agency, *Shukuhaku Ryoko Tokei Chosa* (Statistical Survey on Overnight Travels) January 20, 2016 (in Japanese) (http://www.mlit.go.jp/kankocho/en/siryou/toukei/index.html).

PART IV

Administrative Reforms: Public Service Sectors for the Elderly

CHAPTER 10

Local Government Financing of Health Insurance and the Revitalization—Facilitating Migration of the Elderly

Wataru Suzuki

Abstract The decline in Japan's birth rate, the most rapid in the world, and the aging of its population are not uniform throughout the country. The number of elderly residents of Japan's regional areas has already begun to decline, while those numbers in Tokyo and other large cities will surge in the future. Because prices are regulated in Japan's medical and nursing care sectors, we cannot rely on the adjustment of supply and demand based on the price mechanism. The Japanese government should implement measures to correct the uneven regional distribution on the demand side by promoting migration of the nation's elderly population to regional areas. This chapter proposes reforms to the National Health Insurance and nursing care insurance systems, which currently hinder the movement of Japan's elderly citizens to regional areas.

Keywords Regional revitalization • National Health Insurance • Long-term care insurance • Soft budget constraints • Regulatory reform • Risk adjustment

W. Suzuki (✉)
Faculty of Economics, Gakushuin University, Tokyo, Japan

T. Hatta (ed.), *Economic Challenges Facing Japan's Regional Areas*,
https://doi.org/10.1007/978-981-10-7110-2_10

The Abe administration has initiated a policy of "regional revitalization" as a new economic policy seeking to correct the overconcentration of population and economic activity in Tokyo and arrest the population decline in areas where it is feared that small municipalities might cease to exist. At present, a variety of measures, including the establishment of new subsidies for regional municipalities, the introduction of tax incentives for companies which transfer their head office functions from Tokyo to a regional area, and the transfer of government agencies to regional areas are either under review or being implemented. Of these, however, the most effective and the most practical policy is the promotion of the movement of members of Japan's elderly population to the nation's regional areas.

Under this policy, the movement of seniors currently living in cities to regional areas while they are still healthy would directly arrest the decline in the population of those areas, and in the near future their demand for medical and nursing care would both maintain and create employment opportunities for young people in the same areas. This is a "win–win" situation both for large metropolises and for Japan's regional areas.

The advantages for the nation's regions are clear. As the agricultural, forestry, and manufacturing industries in Japan's regions have declined, it has been service industries targeting the elderly, such as medical and nursing care, which have provided employment opportunities for local young people. However, the elderly population in the majority of Japan's regions is either already beginning to decline or expected to decline in the near future, which will make the medical and nursing care staff and facilities which have been maintained up to the present unnecessary. With the decline in the elderly population, the last remaining young human resources, who had previously worked as nursing and medical care staff, in particular young women, will migrate to the cities, accelerating the decline in the regional birth rate, and raising the real possibility that some regional municipalities will die out. Alarm bells were raised regarding this possibility by the Masuda Report (Japan Policy Council, 2014), which sent shock waves through Japanese society. The movement of elderly citizens to regional areas could help to arrest this trend.

At the same time, the policy also has significant merit for Japan's cities. In large cities such as Tokyo and Osaka, the fact that many elderly residents are on waiting lists to enter aged care facilities is already a social problem. With the rapid aging of the population in the nation's cities, this problem is expected to increase in severity in the future. Establishing the necessary number of new care facilities in cities such as Tokyo and Osaka, where land prices are high, will entail the investment of an enormous amount of public funds. By contrast, if we were able to promote the movement of the nation's elderly population to regional areas, we could make use of facilities that were no longer in use, or establish facilities in areas in which land and labor were cheap. This would represent a considerable fiscal savings throughout the nation. Naturally, the policy would not be urged on people who felt no desire to move. However, many among Japan's baby boom generation were born in regional areas, and for these elderly citizens, the move to a region boasting an adequate medical and nursing care infrastructure could represent an appealing choice, as a return home. With the backing of government policy, this could have the potential to stem the flow of people from Japan's regional areas.

The greatest obstacle to the movement of members of the elderly population to regional areas is the issue of municipal funding of medical and nursing care, as indicated by Hatta (1996, 2015) and Suzuki (2015). When elderly people move from a city to a regional area, they join the National Health Insurance and nursing care insurance programs in their new municipality. However, because a very low burden of payment of health and nursing care insurance fees is placed on the elderly in Japan, their actual medical and nursing care expenses significantly exceed the premiums paid. The movement of elderly people to a municipality therefore increases the burden of payment for the municipal administration, and insurance premiums for residents increase. For this reason, elderly people moving from cities represent a burden to municipalities, which are therefore understandably halfhearted about accepting them. As Hayashi (2018) points out in Chap. 12, municipalities attempt to block the movement of elderly people to their areas by refusing to grant permission for the construction of new nursing care facilities.

However, taking Japan as a whole into consideration, the movement of the elderly from cities to regional areas should not change the overall burden that they represent. If the movement of the elderly increases the burden in regional areas, it also reduces the burden in cities. The essence of the problem is that the current National Health Insurance and nursing care insurance systems function as "regional (i.e. 'local') insurance," and are not portable; because of this, the movement of the elderly from cities imposes a burden on regional areas.

The *jukyochi tokurei* system provides a partial solution to this problem. Under this system, the burden of medical and nursing care expenses for elderly people who move to a regional area and enter a long-term care insurance facility are borne by the municipality from which the individual has moved (for example, one of Tokyo's wards). However, this system has limitations, in that it only applies to elderly people who enter regional institutions, and not to those living in normal residences.

Tokushima, Kochi, and Akita prefectures are currently proposing the conditional expansion of *jukyochi tokurei* privileges to elderly people who move into normal residences in areas designated as National Strategic Special Zones. However, this proposal is facing strong opposition from the Ministry of Health, Labour and Welfare, which believes that it runs counter to the principle of "regional insurance," and discussions concerning this so-called "bedrock regulation" have reached an impasse.

However, we do have available a proposal for fundamental reform which will (1) maintain the framework of "regional insurance"; (2) not impede the movement of elderly people to regional areas; (3) correct disparities in the burden of National Health Insurance and nursing care insurance premiums between municipalities; and (4) enable small municipalities to achieve fiscal stability. This idea would kill four birds with one stone. In essence, this proposal would produce a mechanism whereby average per person medical and nursing care costs for each age stratum would be calculated for the entire country, and the national government would provide each municipality with funding to cover "model benefits" or "standardized expenses" (average cost of medical and nursing care per age stratum × number of residents of the municipality in each age stratum) tailored to its specific age makeup. This would mean that no additional fiscal burden would accrue to municipalities with the movement of elderly people to their areas, and that regional areas would therefore welcome an influx of the elderly. A mechanism by means of which insurance premium and taxation rates were calculated to cover the total cost of medical and nursing care for the nation as a whole, and were levied uniformly throughout the country based on the income level and age makeup of the specific region, would represent a fair system. If a municipality were negligent in initiatives such as conducting checks of medical institutions or implementing activities to promote better health among its residents, and the cost of medical and nursing care increased above the calculated model benefits or standardized expenses, insurance rates would increase by the necessary amount in that municipality alone.

This reform was originally proposed by Iwamoto (1996) as a way to solve the fiscal crisis of the health insurance system, and by Hatta (1996) as a way to remove impediments for efficient migration created by the nursing care insurance.

In Chap. 13, Hatta (2018) elucidates the proposal and estimates that the "the model benefit" or "standardized expense" for the national health insurance would be 125,000 yen for each additional resident younger than 65, and 556,000 yen for each additional resident older than 65.

In Chap. 11, Iwamoto (2018) outlines his proposal as "risk adjustment" between municipalities. However, because the law of large numbers does not function effectively in relation to small municipalities, if risk adjustment as described above were implemented, risk from small insurers would remain, as Hayashi (2018) points out in Chap. 12. The system of risk adjustment would be completed by the institution of a system of reinsurance in order to address this problem.

As Hayashi (2018) discusses in detail in Chap. 12, a variety of systems of fiscal adjustment and subsidies already exist within the current regional insurance framework, the purpose of which is to ensure fiscal stability for small municipalities and to reduce disparities in burden between municipalities (Hayashi, 2018). However, these are an aggregate of exceptional measures and small-scale policy responses that are added to every time a problem arises, and they now represent a highly complex patchwork. Because they have involved no fundamental change in design concepts, they also produce insufficient effect. An even greater problem is the fact that these fiscal adjustment and subsidy systems also adjust for factors other than differences in age makeup and income levels between municipalities, which results in laxness in the fiscal management of insurance by the municipalities. In economics, this is known as the problem of soft budget constraint. The discussions underway towards the reform of Japan's system of medical care are seeking to expand the domain of insurance from the village, town, and city level to the prefectural level, but there is a possibility that this might encourage soft budgets.

By contrast, the introduction of the risk adjustment method would maintain the current municipalities as the managing entities while making it possible to adjust differences in age makeup and income level as if the management of insurance were centralized for the entire nation, but without resulting in a relaxation of fiscal discipline by municipalities.

A rapidly declining birth rate and aging population, in addition to overall population decline, is shaking the foundations of Japan's "regional insurance system," and it is clear that it has become impossible to respond using the stopgap measures that have been applied to date. From the perspective of the reform of Japan's social security system as well, it is time to fundamentally address the problems through the introduction of risk adjustment. However, it would be difficult for adjustments between parties with vested interests to be administered by the Ministry of Health, Labour and Welfare, which is constrained in this area. In order to realize regional revitalization that transcends the framework of specific government agencies, it will be necessary to plan comprehensive adjustment that represents the overall optimum under political leadership. At the same time, it will be essential to remember that if the Abe government's regional revitalization policy does not go beyond mere regulatory reform and fiscal allocations to the regions to take in reform of the social security system, it will fail to bear fruit.

References

Hatta, Tatsuo (1996), "*Remark*," in Hatta, T. et al. (eds.), Fukushi wa Toushi Dearu (Welfare is an Investment), Nihon Hyoron Sha Press, pp. 172–173.

Hatta, Tatsuo (2015), "*Chiho soseisaku o tou (Ge): Iju shoheki teppai koso senketsu* (Scrutinizing the Regional Revitalization Policy (Part 2): The First Issue is the Removal of Barriers to Internal Migration)," *Keizai Kyoshitsu*, Nihon Keizai Shimbun Morning Edition, February 6, 2015 (in Japanese).

Hatta, Tatsuo (2018), "Provision of National Health Insurance "Model Benefits" to Japan's Prefectures," in T. Hatta (ed.), *Economic Challenges Facing Japan's Regional Areas*, Plagrave Macmillan, pp. 115–128.

Hayashi, Masayoshi (2018), "Health Care, Long-term Care, and Local Public Finances: Intergovernmental Financing of Social Insurance Programs," in T. Hatta (ed.), *Economic Challenges Facing Japan's Regional Areas*, Plagrave Macmillan, pp. 103–113..

Iwamoto, Yasushi (1996), "Shian: Iryohokenseido Ichigenka (Designing an Integration of Health Insurance Groups)," *Nihon Keizai Kenkyu (JCER Economic Journal)*, No. 33, November, pp. 119–142 (included in Hatta, T. and Yashiro, N. (eds.) (1998), "*Shakaihoken Kaikaku (Social Insurance Reforms)*," Series Gendai Keizai Kenkyu Vol. 16 (Contemporary Economic Study Series Vol. 16), Nihon Keizai Shimbun) (in Japanese).

Iwamoto, Yasushi (2018), "Designing New Systems Through Risk Adjustment," in T. Hatta (ed.), *Economic Challenges Facing Japan's Regional Areas*, Plagrave Macmillan, pp. 99–102.

Japan Policy Council (2014), *Sutoppu shoshika / chiho genki senryaku* (Strategies for Boosting Japan's Birth Rate and Reviving its Regions), May 8, 2014 (www.policycouncil.jp/pdf/prop03/prop03.pdf) (in Japanese).

Suzuki, Wataru (2015), "*Shakai hosho kaikaku no shiten (Jo): "Kongo kaigo" de rodoryoku kakuho o tokuyo no toji kaikaku isoge koreisha no chiho iju o sokushin* (Perspectives on Social Security Reform (Part 1): Secure a Labor Force for "Mixed Care" and Reform the Administration of Intensive-care Old People's Homes to Encourage the Movement of the Elderly to Japan's Regions)," *Keizai Kyoshitsu*, Nihon Keizai Shimbun Morning Edition, April 6, 2015 (in Japanese).

CHAPTER 11

Designing New Systems Through Risk Adjustment

Yasushi Iwamoto

Abstract Public health insurance for Japan's working generations is divided into several systems. There are disparities among these systems in terms of their state of financing due to differences in the income level of premium payers. The state of financing of National Health Insurance is particularly problematic. Risk adjustment can adjust disparities in premiums without hindering the management efforts of insurers. This would make it possible to adjust disparities in premiums arising from factors such as the age structure and income level of subscribers, which cannot be controlled by insurers, while disparities due to other factors would still occur. The introduction of risk adjustment to the National Health Insurance system could be expected to resolve the system's financial problems.

Keywords Public health insurance • *Kyokai Kenpo* • National Health Insurance • Disparity in financing • Risk adjustment • Age-related risk • Incentive for insurers • Reduction of medical costs

Y. Iwamoto (✉)
Graduate School of Economics, University of Tokyo, Tokyo, Japan

T. Hatta (ed.), *Economic Challenges Facing Japan's Regional Areas*,
https://doi.org/10.1007/978-981-10-7110-2_11

Public health insurance for Japan's working generations can be divided into association-managed health insurance for employees of large corporations, health insurance managed by the Japan Health Insurance Association, or "*Kyokai Kenpo*," for employees of small and medium-sized enterprises, mutual aid association insurance for civil servants, and National Health Insurance for the self-employed and unemployed. Because the financing of these forms of health insurance is fundamentally independent, there are disparities in their state of financing due to differences in the income level of the premium payers. The financing of association-managed health insurance and mutual aid association insurance is comparatively stable, but the financial status of *Kyokai Kenpo* insurance is poorer than that of association-managed health insurance, and the state of financing of National Health Insurance is even more problematic.

In addition to the significant disparity in financing among public health insurance systems, there are also disparities within the systems themselves. The maximum disparity in National Health Insurance premiums between different prefectures is 2.6 times. Even within the association-managed insurance system, when the average income of insurees is low, there is no choice but to increase the premium rate in order to ensure a sufficient source of funds for benefit payments.

Financial adjustment mechanisms have been introduced in order to reduce the disparities originating in the independent financing of Japan's health insurance systems. For example, the government and prefectures share the burden of the public funding of the National Health Insurance system. Prefectures bear 9% of the burden of benefit expenses (by means of financial adjustment subsidies), and prefectures and municipalities share the burden of reinsurance programs for high-cost medical treatment and measures to reduce insurance premiums for low-income individuals, to a total of approximately 1.28 trillion yen (as of the FY 2014 closing of accounts). In addition, local administrations have supplemented the National Health Insurance deficit from their general accounts to a total of approximately 380 billion yen (as of the FY 2014 closing of accounts).

Nevertheless, despite these adjustment measures, the disparities in premium payments discussed above continue to exist. The reason for this is that at present, financial adjustment measures are applied only system by system, because the application of universal measures which would entirely eliminate such disparities would also have a negative impact on incentives for insurers to make improvements that would reduce medical expenses.

However, it would in fact be possible to fundamentally correct disparities in premium payments without affecting incentives for insurers. The *Kyokai Kenpo* system provides us with an example of how to do so. Workers and their dependent family members throughout the country are members of the *Kyokai Kenpo* system. Branches in each of the nation's prefectures are the basic administrative units, and insurance premiums differ between prefectures. This mechanism incorporates the concept of risk adjustment.

Because the cost of medical treatment increases as the age of the members of the medical insurance system (with the exception of children) increases, under conditions of independent financing, a high proportion of seniors among the members would necessitate an increase in premiums. In addition, because there are disparities between prefectures in terms of the income level of insurees, under a system of independent financing, premium rates would be extremely high in Okinawa, and extremely low in Tokyo.

The difference in medical costs between prefectures can be divided into (1) a component that can be explained by differences in the age makeup of residents, (2) a component that can be explained by differences in the income levels of residents, and (3) a component that cannot be explained by either. Financial adjustment is therefore conducted in order to ensure that premium rates do not differ due to factors (1) and (2). This is risk adjustment. Factor (3) is a result of the independent financing of the systems, and remains reflected in premium rates.

Risk adjustment adjusts disparities in premiums without hindering the management efforts of insurers. This makes it possible to adjust disparities in premiums arising from factors such as the age structure and income level of members, which cannot be controlled by insurers, while disparities due to other factors still occur. If insurers make efforts to reduce premiums resulting from these other factors, the outcomes will not be passed on to other insurance systems, but their benefits will be enjoyed within the original system.

In 1996, the author proposed introducing risk adjustment to all of Japan's health insurance systems. The practical advantage offered by this proposal was that disparities in premiums could be corrected with no need to amalgamate the existing multiple systems, and transitional costs would be low. It would be necessary to introduce a system for the adjustment of finances between the insurance systems, but there is already a mechanism for financial adjustment in relation to 65–74 year olds which could function as the infrastructure for financial adjustment for the systems overall. This mechanism could be improved and put into effect.

Even if risk adjustment cannot be introduced at once to all of Japan's public health insurance systems, it would be possible to expand its application in stages from the *Kyokai Kenpo* system to the other systems. For example, based on the National Health Insurance Reform Act established in FY 2015, risk adjustment will be introduced to the system from FY 2018. There has been no fundamental risk adjustment in relation to age-related risk in the National Health Insurance system up to the present. Because of this, there are significant disparities in premiums. However, because the current system of financial adjustment applied to National Health Insurance is reflected to a considerable extent in benefit payments, there is little incentive for insurers to make efforts to reduce medical costs.

The introduction of risk adjustment to the National Health Insurance system can be expected to reduce disparities in insurance premiums and promote management initiatives on the part of insurers.

Reference

Iwamoto, Yasushi (1996), "*Shian: Iryohokenseido Ichigenka* (Designing an Integration of Health Insurance Groups)," *Nihon Keizai Kenkyu* (JCER Economic Journal), No. 33, November, pp. 119–142 (included in Hatta, Tatsuo, and Yashiro, Naohiro (eds.) (1998), "*Shakaihoken Kaikaku* (Social Insurance Reforms)," *Shirizu gendai keizai kenkyu* 16 (Contemporary Economic Study Series Vol. 16), Nihon Keizai Shimbun) (in Japanese).

CHAPTER 12

Health Care, Long-term Care, and Local Public Finances: Intergovernmental Financing of Social Insurance Programs

Masayoshi Hayashi

Abstract Local governments form an integral part of the Japanese system of health and long-term care for the elderly. In particular, municipalities (cities, towns, and villages) manage National Health Insurance (NHI) programs and Long-term Care Insurance (LTCI) programs for their elderly residents. Furthermore, all municipalities within a given prefecture form an administrative unit which finances the costs of medical benefits for those aged 75 and above. This chapter offers a brief overview of the role of local governments in financing NHI and LTCI benefits. In addition, it discusses some of the policy issues that the NHI and LTCI systems are facing, including compromised horizontal equity, potential failure to pool risks, and adverse incentives for municipalities to ration social services.

Keywords Intergovernmental relations • Long-term care • Public health insurance • Long-term Care Insurance • National Health Insurance • Regional insurance

---

M. Hayashi (✉)
Faculty & Graduate School of Economics, University of Tokyo, Tokyo, Japan

T. Hatta (ed.), *Economic Challenges Facing Japan's Regional Areas*,
https://doi.org/10.1007/978-981-10-7110-2_12

1 Introduction

Local governments form an integral part of the Japanese system of health and long-term care for the elderly. While the central government designs the care system, local governments play other important roles. In particular, municipalities (cities, towns, and villages) manage National Health Insurance (NHI) programs and Long-term Care Insurance (LTCI) programs for their elderly residents. Municipalities also conduct eligibility assessments for LTCI benefits and control the supply of long-term care (LTC) services. In addition, all municipalities within a given prefecture form an administrative unit that finances the costs of medical benefits for those aged 75 and above (the cohort known as "old-old"). This chapter, focusing on NHI and LTCI, provides background information concerning the role of local governments in financing health and long-term care for the elderly in Japan, and briefly discusses some of the issues that these systems are facing. These issues include compromised horizontal equity among municipalities, potential failure to pool risks within municipalities, and possible adverse incentives for municipalities to ration social services that may result in inefficient allocation of social service resources.

2 National Health Insurance: Overview of the System and Current Issues

2.1 Provision of Health Care Benefits in Japan

The benefits side of the Japanese system of public health care is universal and uniform. The system provides the entire population with standardized benefits that cover a wide range of medical services and prescribed drugs. Patients are free to choose any health care service provider. With some exceptions, copayments and coverage for services are identical regardless of the type of provider (clinic or hospital, private or public). This also applies to prescribed drugs. The copayment rate is 30 %, with reductions for the elderly with incomes below a specific threshold: 20 % for those aged 70–74 and 10 % for those aged 75 and above. In addition, there are ceilings on copayments for catastrophic expenditures.

In standard cases, providers receive payment for the health care services and prescribed drugs they provide (i.e., retrospective payment). Following the fee schedule set by the central government, they collect copayments directly from their patients, and receive reimbursements for the residual costs from insurers. The insurers finance the reimbursed portion of the medical expenses, that is, the insurance benefits.

2.2 *How are NHI Programs Financed?*

Different public health insurance programs finance such public health insurance benefits. Table 12.1 summarizes these programs, including the NHI. The NHI is a residence-based insurance scheme managed by municipalities acting as insurers. Residents of the municipality who are excluded from Employees' Health Insurance (EHI) programs are enrolled in the

Table 12.1 Public health insurance programs in Japan

Type			*Insurer (No.)*	*Coverage*
Employees' Health Insurance	JHIA-managed		Japan Health Insurance Association (JHIA)	35 million
	Association-managed		Employees' health insurance associations (1431)	29 million
	Seamen's Health Insurance		Japan Health Insurance Association (1)	0.13 million
	Mutual Aid Association Insurance	Central government employees	Mutual aid associations (20)	9 million
		Local government employees	Mutual aid associations (64)	
		Private school teachers and employees	Private School Teachers and Employees Association (1)	
National Health Insurance			Municipalities (1717) National Health Insurance Associations (164)*	42 million
Health Care Service for the Old-Old			Prefecture-wide large-area unions (47)	13 million

Note: As of April 2015

Source: Various documents provided by the Ministry of Health, Labour and Welfare

*Self-employed professionals such as doctors and lawyers have opted out of the municipal NHI programs to form their own NHI associations. In the text, the term NHI refers to the municipal NHI, excluding the NHI associations

NHI program. These typically include the unemployed, the self-employed, farmers, and employees of smaller firms and their families. Individuals enrolled in the NHI pay premiums to the municipality in which they reside. The premium schedule consists of several components. The central government sets the menu for these components, and premiums depend on household income, assets, and size. However, the menu is also broad enough to allow municipalities to establish their own premium schedules.

Elderly citizens aged 65–74 (the cohort known as "young-old") represent about 30 % of total NHI enrollments. Because this stratum tends to have more medical needs and earn less than the younger working population, Japan's elderly are placing fiscal stress on municipal NHI finances. A high proportion of the unhealthy leads to an increase in medical needs, while a high proportion of the poor results in a decline in premium collections due to reductions in premiums for low-income households.

Layers of transfers of funds therefore help municipalities finance their NHI benefits. First, there are two schemes of nationwide cost sharing which in effect transfer funds from EHI programs to NHI programs. One scheme, known as the Expense Grant for the Young-Old (EGYO), addresses medical costs for citizens aged 65–74. Because the majority of those aged 65–74 are enrolled in the NHI, municipalities receive net transfers from this cost-sharing scheme. Another scheme also transfers funds from EHI programs to the NHI to cover benefits for individuals who have transferred from EHI programs due to having retired before the age of 65.

Second, a prefecture-wide scheme, the Collective Stabilization Program (CSP), equalizes and stabilizes municipal revenue streams. The CSP disburses grants that match 59 % of actual NHI benefits (net of the EGYO). Municipalities contribute amounts to the program that in aggregate equal the total amount of the CSP grants. For benefits below 800,000 yen per receipt, the municipal share of the contribution is set at the average value of the municipal share of NHI enrollments and NHI benefits (net of the EGYO). For benefits above 800,000 yen (i.e., catastrophic expenses), the municipal share is simply the municipal share of NHI benefits.

Third, the central and prefectural governments provide subsidies from their general budgets. The central government subsidies include the Medical Benefit Subsidy (a grant corresponding to 32 % of NHI benefits) and the CSP Subsidy (a grant corresponding to 25 % of municipal contributions to the CSP). The central government also allocates funds corresponding to 9% of the total NHI benefits to the Adjustment Grant (AG), which addresses fiscal disparities among municipalities. The prefectural subsidies parallel their central government counterparts with a grant corresponding to 25% of municipal CSP contributions and a prefectural version of the AG that allocates funds equivalent to 9% of the benefits aggregated at the prefectural level.

Lastly, municipalities make intra-municipal transfers from their general accounts to their NHI special accounts. Such transfers consist of two types. One is statutory; set by national laws, it compensates for revenue losses due to premium reductions for the poor, and benefit increases caused by special circumstances that municipalities cannot control. The other is discretionary. Such transfers arguably function as ex post subsidies that make up deficits when other types of funding, including increasing premiums, are not available.

2.3 Fiscal Disparities and Compromise in Horizontal Equity

Figure 12.1 shows the distribution of premiums and benefits per enrollment for each municipality in 2010. As this figure shows, significant fiscal disparities still exist among municipalities: the system of fiscal transfers is

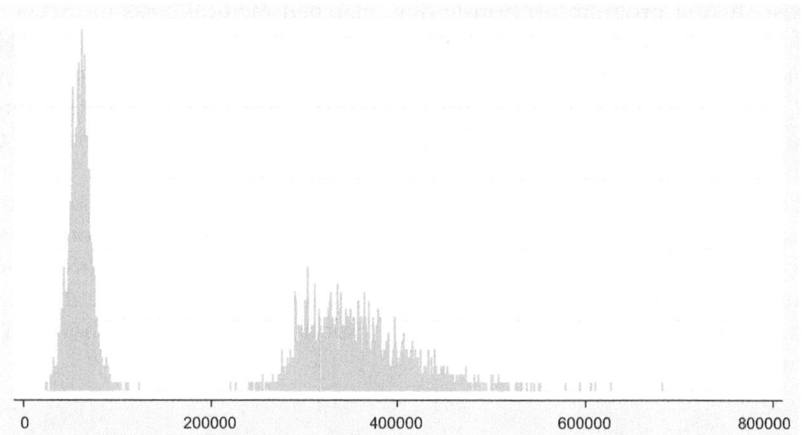

Fig. 12.1 Distribution of per enrollment NHI premiums and benefits (2010). Note: The histogram on the left-hand side shows the distribution of NHI premiums per enrollment; the histogram on the right-hand side shows the distribution of NHI benefits per enrollment. Source: Annual Survey on the National Health Insurance Programs, 2010 (*Heisei 24 nendo Kokumin Kenko Hoken Jigyo Nenpo*). The Ministry of Health, Labour and Welfare

not sufficient to address the uneven spatial distribution of the unhealthy and the poor among municipalities. Kitaura (2007) examined the issue of disparities among NHI programs by laboriously calculating annual premiums for a couple with identical income in every municipality. He showed that the premiums for a couple with a typical annual income for the elderly (2.3 million yen) would range from around 60,000–400,000 yen depending on the municipality. This clearly demonstrates that horizontal equity among NHI programs is significantly compromised.

Another problem with the NHI is the size of its individual programs. Many municipalities are too small to pool risk (Hayashi 2012). In 2010, half of all municipalities had fewer than 7800 enrollments, and a quarter had fewer than 3100. In small municipalities, we may readily predict unexpected hikes in NHI benefits. Such hikes have to be covered by either an increase in premiums or ex post intra-municipal transfers from the municipal general account. Since an increase in the premiums is usually avoided, this leads to a further increase in intra-municipal transfers, imposing further restrictions on municipal expenditures in general budgets.

Given these concerns, the central government is trying to integrate municipal NHI programs at the prefectural level. In fact, the prefectural cost-sharing program previously only matched medical costs in excess of 300,000 yen per receipt, but has matched all cost ranges since 2015. Furthermore, starting in 2018, prefectures will involve themselves more directly in NHI programs by distributing the cost of NHI benefits among municipalities. Each municipality will contribute the specified amount to the prefectural administration, which will then finance the NHI benefits. This new system may smooth disparities and ease the fluctuation of current NHI expenses among municipalities. Nevertheless, it will not help to solve the disparities *among prefectures* themselves. Furthermore, since municipalities will still decide their own premiums based on their allocated costs, the system will not effectively respond to the issue of horizontal equity in premium setting either.

3 Long-term Care Insurance: Overview of the System and Current Issues

3.1 Long-term Care Benefits

The LTCI covers persons aged 65 and over (Category I) and persons aged 40–64 (Category II). To receive LTCI benefits, prospective recipients must have their needs assessed by their municipality of residence. The eligible are classified into seven stages according to the severity of their LTC needs, consisting of two stages of Support Required (SR1 and SR2) for the least severe, and five stages of Care Required (CR), from 1 to 5, with 5 being the most severe. The eligible are entitled to "purchase" LTC services from providers of their choice, with copayments amounting to 10% or 20% of the actual cost, depending on individual's income level (i.e. the LTCI benefit covers 80% or 90% of the expense). Benefits are available up to a ceiling, the amount of which increases according to the seven stages of the severity of individual needs. The benefits for Category II are restricted to some specific age-related diseases. In addition, those classified in SR1 and SR2 are not eligible for institutional care. The beneficiaries, if they desire, can self-finance additional services.

3.2 *How Are LTCI Programs Financed?*

The LTCI is another residence-based scheme managed by municipalities. As in the case of NHI benefits, municipalities finance LTCI benefits through their LTCI special accounts, from premiums, cost-sharing schemes, transfers of funds from upper levels of government, and intra-municipal transfers. Municipal residents aged 65 years and over pay the Category I premiums to their municipalities. The rate structure is progressive. It is defined as "an adjustment value × a standard rate," with the adjustment value being larger for higher-income households. While the central government sets out the adjustment values, municipalities set the standard rates. When setting this rate, they forecast their LTCI benefits and revenues for a three-year period, termed the Program Management Period. In particular, they set their standard rate such that Category I premiums balance their three-year budget.

Since the local premiums are not sufficient to finance LTCI benefits, as in the case of the NHI, various layers of transfers of funds provide fiscal assistance to municipal LTCI programs. First, Category II premiums paid by individuals aged 40–64 are pooled in a national fund and then allocated to municipal programs. This grant, called the Fee Payment Fund Grant, matches 28% of LTCI benefits. It thus works as an equalizing device, as it favors municipalities in which the Category II share is smaller and LTCI benefits are larger.

Second, there are two prefecture-wide schemes for cost sharing. One is the Mutual Stabilization Program, the intention of which is to equalize and stabilize municipal LTCI revenues. The other is the Fiscal Stabilization Fund (FSF). Prefectures pool contributions made by municipalities (subsidized by prefectural governments and the central government) to the

FSF, and then use the pool to finance FSF grants or loans to provide fiscal assistance to municipalities that are hit by unexpected revenue losses.

Third, the central and prefectural governments disburse subsidies out of their budgets. Central government subsidies include the Long-term Care Benefits Subsidy, which matches 20 (15)% of in-home (institutional) care benefits, and the Adjustment Subsidy (AS), which allocates central government funds equivalent to 5% of the national total of all LTCI benefits. The latter aims to equalize municipal Category I premiums across municipalities, allowing for the percentage of those aged 75 years and over (i.e., LTC needs) and the average income of those aged 65 and over (i.e., premium bases). At the same time, prefectures cover 12.5 (17.5)% of in-home (institutional) care benefits in their jurisdictions through the Cost-sharing Subsidy.

Finally, another 12.5% of benefits is financed by intra-municipal transfers from the general account to the LTCI special account within a municipality. It should be noted that, unlike the NHI, municipalities are not allowed to make ex post intra-municipal transfers to cover deficits in the LTCI special account.

3.3 Fiscal Disparities and Municipal Incentives to Limit LTCI Benefits

Figure 12.2 shows the distribution of LTCI premiums and benefits per enrollment in 2010. Despite the equalizing effects of the transfers mentioned above, premiums and benefits differ among municipalities. While the spread of the disparities is smaller than in the case of the NHI, they still reflect an uneven spatial distribution of the less healthy and the poor among those aged 65 and older. This also implies that horizontal equity is compromised in LTCI programs just as it is in NHI programs.

Another problem associated with the LTCI is that municipalities may face incentives to restrict LTCI benefits. Given the mechanism for budgeting LTCI expenditures discussed above, increases in LTCI benefits result in corresponding increases in local burdens (i.e., Category I premiums plus intra-municipal transfers) to the extent that the system of transfers fails to offset the increase in benefits. While the offsetting effect of the transfer system may be substantial *on average*, this may not be the case

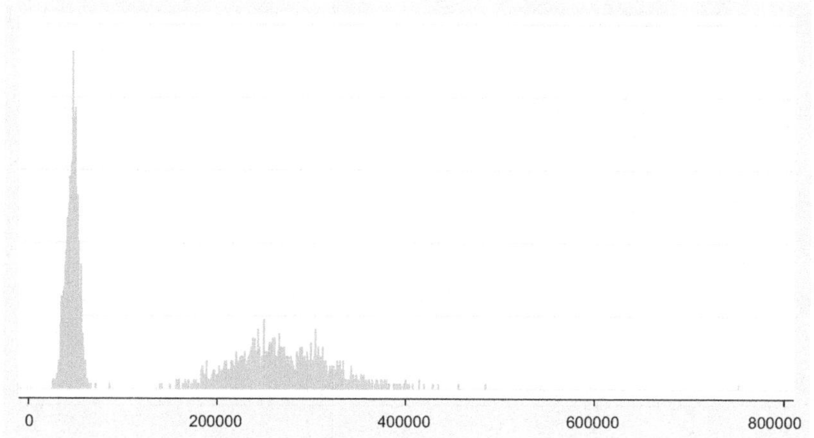

Fig. 12.2 Distribution of per enrollment LTCI premiums and benefits (2010). Note: The histogram on the left-hand side shows the distribution of Category I premiums per enrollment; the histogram on the right-hand side shows the distribution of LTCI benefits per enrollment. Source: Annual Survey on the Long-term Care Insurance Programs, 2010 (*Heisei 22-nendo Kaigo Hoken Jigyo Jokyo Hokoku Nenpo*). The Ministry of Health, Labour and Welfare

for municipalities with smaller populations, or for municipalities with a large proportion of local costs (i.e., municipalities in the upper tail of Fig. 12.3). This may result in two types of adverse effect, as described below.

First, there may be an incentive for municipalities to control demand for LTC services. Because municipalities conduct assessments of the eligibility of LTCI applicants, they may assess the LTC needs of the applicants downward in order to control increases in LTCI benefits. Hayashi and Kazama (2008) provide corroboration for this adverse effect, showing that municipalities with more stringent fiscal climates display a greater tendency to reject applications for LTCI benefits. Second, there may also be an incentive for municipalities to restrict the supply of LTC services. Providers of LTC services can be private or public. If they are private, it is municipalities which grant permission for their operation when they operate within single municipal boundaries. In addition, municipalities sometimes provide institutional

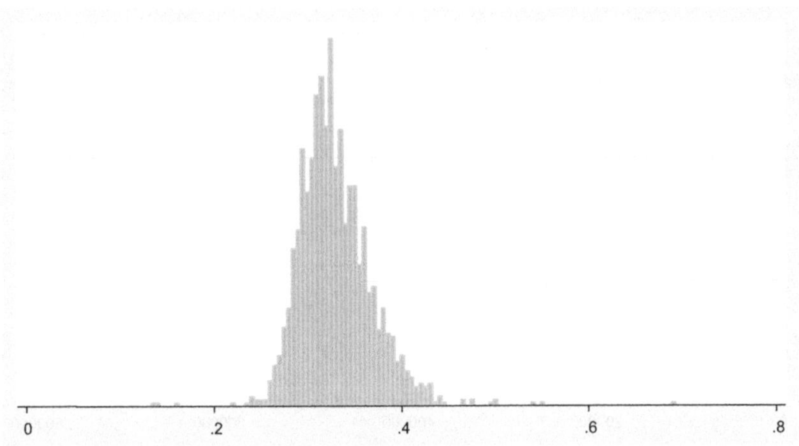

Fig. 12.3 Distribution of municipal cost ratios for LTCI programs (2010). Note: Municipal cost ratio = (Category I premiums + intra-municipal transfers) ÷ LTCI benefits. Source: Annual Survey on the Long-term Care Insurance Programs, 2010 (*Heisei 22-nendo Kaigo Hoken Jigyo Jokyo Hokoku Nenpo*). The Ministry of Health, Labour and Welfare

LTC services themselves. Unlike NHI programs, therefore, municipalities have ample opportunity to control the supply of LTC services, especially in the case of institutional LTC services. Focusing on this incentive aspect, Hatta (2015) argues that municipalities tend to limit the size of institutional LTC services in an attempt to exclude the elderly from their jurisdictions. This is because a growing elderly population would lead to an increased local burden in terms of the LTCI and NHI budgets, especially for small municipalities in rural areas. Hatta also argues that rural municipalities that adopt this type of "policy of exclusion" contribute to inefficient resource allocation, given that they are likely to possess a comparative advantage in providing institutional LTC services because of their low land prices. In addition, according to Hatta, they forgo opportunities to increase local employment with increased LTC service provision.

4 Concluding Remarks

Given the institutional complexities of the NHI and the LTCI, and their significance for local public finance in an aging Japan, the present space is too limited to properly delineate the problems and future prospects of

Japan's two residence-based systems of social insurance. There is also unfortunately no single reference that could provide a comprehensive overview of these topics. Readers may nevertheless obtain some useful information from Olivares-Tirado and Tamiya (2014) concerning the LTCI programs, and Mochida (2008) concerning local public finance in Japan.

References

Hatta, Tatsuo (2015), Chiho Sosei saku wo tou (ge): Iju no shogai teppai koso senketsu (On the Chiho-Sosei policy (part II): The priority is removing barriers to internal migration) *Nihon Keizai Shimbun*, Morning Edition, 2015/02/06 (in Japanese).

Hayashi, Masayoshi (2012), "Channels of stabilization in a system of local public health insurance: the case of the National Health Insurance in Japan," CIRJE-F-847, Faculty of Economics, University of Tokyo.

Hayashi, Masayoshi, & Kazama, Haruka (2008), "Horizontal equity or gatekeeping? Fiscal effects on eligibility assessments for long-term care insurance programs in Japan," *Asia-Pacific Journal of Accounting and Economics* 15(3), 257–276.

Kitaura, Yoshiro (2007), *Kokuminkenko hokenryo (zei) no suiheiteki fubyodosei* (Horizontal Equity in the National Health Insurance Premiums). KISER Discussion Paper Series No.8, 2007/9 (in Japanese).

Mochida, Nobuki (2008), *Fiscal Decentralization and Local Public Finance in Japan*. Routledge.

Olivares-Tirado, Pedro, & Tamiya, Nanako (2014), *Trends and Factors in Japan's Long-Term Care Insurance System*. Springer.

CHAPTER 13

Provision of National Health Insurance "Model Benefits" to Japan's Prefectures

Tatsuo Hatta

Abstract Regional areas, in which land rents are relatively low, clearly possess a comparative advantage in the provision of elderly services. Nevertheless, regional municipalities do not welcome influxes of elderly residents, because such influxes disadvantage regional municipal governments by requiring them to shoulder a considerable financial burden for social security while providing virtually no increase in local tax revenues.

Influxes of elderly residents would be stimulated if the national government paid an amount corresponding to a "model benefit" for each insurance subscriber, based on the average per person benefit for that age cohort throughout the entire country.

The present chapter estimates that the model benefit would be 125,000 yen for each additional resident younger than 65, and 556,000 yen for each additional resident older than 65.

Keywords Efficient allocation of resources • Inflow of elderly residents • Model benefits • National Health Insurance • Reallocation of the number of hospital beds • Social insurance for the elderly

T. Hatta (✉)
Asian Growth Research Institute, Kitakyushu, Fukuoka, Japan

T. Hatta (ed.), *Economic Challenges Facing Japan's Regional Areas*,
https://doi.org/10.1007/978-981-10-7110-2_13

1 Objective of the Present Chapter

The national and local governments in Japan share the burden of fiscal expenditure to fund social insurance for the elderly.[1] However, the system currently in effect has led to inefficient allocation of resources. This chapter analyzes how to reform this system of financing services for the elderly. Estimation of the amount of proposed "model benefits" to be provided by the national government to eliminate the misallocation of resources is a particular focus of the chapter.

Under Japan's current system, local governments must finance a certain portion of elderly residents' age-related social expenses (medical care, nursing, etc.), despite the fact that the elderly residents contribute almost no tax revenue to these administrations. On average, elderly residents produce a deficit for local governments, which results in two problems.

The first is that a local government with a large number of elderly residents is compelled to bear a significant fiscal burden for social services for the elderly, as a result of which it may be forced to curtail other local services. This situation could even lead to a population outflow.

The second is that this fiscal burden provides a disincentive to local governments to approve the construction of adequate facilities in their Elderly Welfare Plans. As a result, while elderly citizens may wish to move from large cities to rural areas, for example because they were born there or the weather is warmer, such moves are discouraged.[2]

A number of researchers have conducted research on the division of roles between the national and local governments in relation to medical and nursing care for the elderly. In particular, Iwamoto (1996, 1998, 2015) Hatta (1996, pp. 172–3; 2015a, 2016a, 2016b) and Suzuki (2010, 2015) suggest that if the national government directly financed the expense of medical care for the elderly by providing model benefits, local governments would no longer be motivated to impede the inflow of elderly residents.

Under this system, if the amount of model benefits provided by the national government to a prefecture exceeded the amount of actual benefits paid in the prefecture, the prefecture would be able to use the surplus at its own discretion; as a result, the greater the inflow of elderly residents, the greater the improvement in the fiscal condition of the local government concerned. Because an inflow of elderly residents would benefit the local economy through, for example, increased spending of pension benefits, local governments' incentives to inhibit inflows of the elderly would disappear. The new system would also motivate local governments to control benefit expenditure, for example through preventative measures.

This chapter estimates two types of model benefits to be provided by the national government to local governments in order to assist in the realization of this policy goal.

First, it estimates model benefits to be provided to local governments based on the specific attributes of residents of the municipalities concerned. The analysis conducted in this paper indicates that each additional resident aged 64 or below would increase annual National Health Insurance benefits by an average of 125,000 yen, and each additional resident aged above 64 would increase benefits by an average of 556,000 yen. These model benefits will be termed "age-specific per person model benefits" (APMB). Under the new system, the national government would provide a grant to each prefecture in an amount equal to the product of APMB and the size of the population in each age cohort in that prefecture to finance National Health Insurance expenditure. If this system were introduced, the average per person grant provided by the national government to the prefectures would increase as the ratio of elderly residents in the prefecture increased, eliminating the incentive on the part of the prefectures to control the inflow of elderly residents.

However, the difference between the model benefits estimated in this way and actual National Health Insurance expenditure would be very large for some prefectures, including Saga Prefecture, Nagasaki Prefecture, and Kagoshima Prefecture. These prefectures would be required to supplement expenditure by more than 70,000 yen per person annually. Because this would represent a significant fiscal burden for local governments, some form of transitional measure may be necessary to allow adjustment in the initial stage of introduction of a model benefit system.

Next, therefore, the chapter estimates the amount of "transitional model benefits" to be provided by the national government to local governments during the phase of adjustment to the new system. This estimation takes into consideration the number of hospital beds allocated to each prefecture, a figure which has a strong influence on the current insurance benefit expenditure in each. The transitional model benefits would represent the amount of model benefits to be applied during the process of transition, until the application of the APMB (which would be based solely on the attributes of recipients).

2 Comparative Advantages of Regional Areas

Which industries can enable regional economies to grow?

In addition to primary industry, regional areas possess comparative advantages in the elderly services industry.

Residences, nursing facilities, and medical care facilities can be built at very low cost in regional cities because land prices are lower there than in huge metropolises. The average cost of residential land in Japan's rural areas is approximately 31,000 yen per square meter, compared with approximately 195,000 per square meter in the Tokyo metropolitan area. Migration to rural areas would, therefore, enable Japan's elderly population to lead more comfortable lives.

It would also represent considerable savings in terms of the nation's public expenditure on medical and nursing care. Viewed from the government's perspective, regional areas possess a clear comparative advantage over Tokyo for the siting of facilities for the elderly. In addition, because elderly residents would bring with them their entire pensions, as well as other forms of income, an inflow of elderly residents would represent a boon to local economies.

3 Why Local Governments Do Not Welcome Inflows of Elderly Residents

It is natural to assume that the majority of Japan's elderly citizens will wish to continue living in the large cities with which they are familiar. But there are also other elderly people who would like to return to their hometown, or who would like to live the country lifestyle that was unavailable to them when they were working. Despite this, however, only a limited proportion of Japan's elderly population is migrating to rural areas.

The reason for this is rooted in the local public finance system. A local government's tax revenues will barely increase if elderly residents move to a municipality. But the burden on the local government for social services, in particular National Health Insurance, will increase. Under the current system, if the elderly population increases, a local government will not only suffer the burden of expenses for nursing care facilities, but also later for medical care. Because of this, local governments have an incentive to control the migration of elderly residents into their areas.

Local governments in Japan have a policy tool to enable them to do so. The construction of new nursing care facilities will not be approved if it does not accord with the plans for the provision of senior care facilities drawn up by the prefecture. However, prefectural facility construction plans are formulated based on the sum of the plans formulated by the cities, towns, and villages within the prefecture, and local governments are reluctant to actively formulate plans for the provision of facilities for the elderly.

4 Is There a Reason that Japan's Local Governments Are Required to Finance the Burden?

If the National Health Insurance system were reformed to provide local governments with an incentive to welcome elderly residents, the elderly would begin to move away from large metropolitan areas, towards rural areas.

This is clear from the cases of Florida and Arizona in the USA. In the USA, a public health insurance system called Medicare has been providing insurance for citizens aged 65 and over for decades. Because Medicare is a national system, elderly residents do not entail a burden of expense for Florida and Arizona. These states have therefore attempted by every means possible to attract elderly residents. As a result, wealthy elderly people have flowed to both states.

In Japan, unlike the USA, local governments are required to finance some of the expenses for elderly residents. There is a reason for this. If the national government were to assume responsibility for all payments that were actually made, local governments would have no incentive to economize on benefit expenditure. Japan's current system, requiring local governments to fund part of the burden, provides those local governments with powerful incentives to refrain from lavish expenditure in the area of National Health Insurance and to engage in preventative initiatives.

The author therefore proposes that the national government provide each local government with a grant equivalent to the National Health Insurance model benefit, which reflects the specific characteristics of the National Health Insurance subscribers in that local government's administrative region (for example, a national average benefit amount based on the age of each individual). Under this system, if the total amount of actual benefit payments exceeded the total amount of the grant supplied by the national government, the amount in excess would be made up by the local government. On the other hand, if the total amount actually paid out as benefits were lower than the amount of the grant supplied by the national government, as a result of preventative initiatives on the part of the local government, the amount of the saving would be incorporated into the local government's general accounts. This would ultimately provide a stronger incentive for local governments to economize on benefit expenditure by means of preventative initiatives.

5 A National Government-funded "Model Benefit" System for National Health Insurance and its Effects

The proposed reform of the National Health Insurance system can be outlined as follows.

First, the existing local government-based system would be maintained. This would ensure that an incentive for local governments to put preventative initiatives in place would remain.[3]

Second, the national government would finance each local government with model benefits determined on the basis of the characteristics of the National Health Insurance subscribers resident in its administrative region. This would mean that National Health Insurance payments for the elderly would basically be financed by the national government.

Third, the local government would pay the difference between the amount financed by the national government (equal to the model benefits) and the amount actually paid as benefits. This amount could be either positive or negative.

Under this system, the net burden on local governments would be zero, on average. But if, for example, the local government neglected the implementation of preventative measures and as a result medical expenses exceeded the amount of the model benefits supplied for its elderly population, it would be the local government's responsibility to make up the extra amount.

We will term this proposed system a "national government-financed model benefit system for National Health Insurance." Because the implementation of this reform would shift that portion of the financing burden of benefit payments borne by local governments to the national government, it would correct the situation in which cities with large numbers of elderly residents have suffered a relatively heavy financial burden of expenditure on social services for the elderly. However, this reform would not increase the total amount of benefits in Japan as a whole, and hence the total National Health Insurance burden on Japanese citizens as a whole would not increase.

The removal of the National Health Insurance burden on regional cities, towns and villages would have the following effects:

(1) The fiscal status of local governments with a large number of elderly residents would immediately improve.
(2) When elderly citizens moved to regional areas, they would bring their model benefits (determined on the basis of their specific characteristics) with them. Local governments would therefore welcome an inflow of elderly residents. As a result, they would attempt to attract retirees from big cities, for example by inviting tenders for new nursing care facilities.
(3) There would be steady inflows of elderly citizens to regional areas.
(4) This would encourage the migration of young people to regional areas in order to work for the facilities for the elderly, and a virtuous cycle would commence.

6 Estimation of Model Benefits

This section will attempt to estimate the amount of the different model benefits.

Aggregated data will be employed. For the purposes of this estimation, National Health Insurance subscribers will be divided into "elderly subscribers," aged 65 and above, and "young subscribers," aged under 65.[4] We will estimate the APMB for each.[5] For this estimation, the amount of National Health Insurance benefits for each prefecture will be termed B, the number of young subscribers will be termed N^-, and the number of elderly subscribers will be termed N^+. Regression analysis of the benefit per young subscriber, (B/N^-), with respect to the ratio of elderly subscribers to young subscribers, (N^+/N^-), gives the following result.

$$B/N^- = 125 + 556N^+/N^- \quad Adjusted\ R^2 = 0.602 \tag{1}$$
$$(3.226)\ (8.309)$$

It can be seen that as the ratio of elderly subscribers to young subscribers, (N^+/N^-), increases, the benefit per young subscriber, (B/N^-), also increases.

Multiplying both terms of this equation by N^- gives the following.

$$B = 125N^- + 556N^+ \tag{2}$$

This indicates that each additional *young* subscriber would increase annual National Health Insurance benefit payments by 125,000 yen, but each additional *elderly* subscriber would increase annual National Health Insurance benefit payments by 556,000 yen. These numbers represent the APMB for these two age groups. This equation therefore demonstrates that under the current system, an increase in the number of elderly subscribers in a region increases the amount of benefits paid and hence the National Health Insurance burden on the prefecture concerned.

Under the proposed system, the national government would provide APMB amounts for each age stratum of residents of the prefecture concerned. Equation (2) gives the National Health Insurance model benefits for the given number of young subscribers and elderly subscribers in that prefecture.

As pointed out above, those prefectures in which actual expenditure was lower than the grant provided by the national government would be able to use the surplus at their own discretion; local fiscal health would therefore improve as more elderly people moved to the administrative area in question. Because an inflow of elderly residents would benefit the local economy, this reform would eliminate the incentive on the part of local governments to control inflows of the elderly. Unlike the existing scheme, in which local governments are responsible for part of the burden of funding the system, the proposed scheme does not distort the allocation of resources.

Under this system, prefectures could not influence the amount provided by the national government. This would also give the prefectures an incentive to reduce social expenses for the elderly.

7 Estimation of Amount of Transitional Model Benefits

However, if the national government financed prefectural National Health Insurance benefits based on Eq. (2), the difference between the amount of the actual benefit payment and the amount of the grant could be very large. For example, prefectures such as Saga Prefecture, Nagasaki Prefecture, and Kagoshima Prefecture would be forced to make up an amount of 70,000 yen per person per year. This would represent a considerable increase in the fiscal burden on local governments, making some form of transitional measures essential in practice.

In Japan at present, a specific number of hospital beds is allocated to each prefecture. The allocation of hospital beds on a per person basis differs significantly between prefectures. For example, the number of hospital beds allocated per National Health Insurance subscriber aged under 65 in Saitama Prefecture is three times as high as the number allocated in Kochi Prefecture

At the same time, the total amount of National Health Insurance benefits paid per resident is higher in regions with a higher allocation of hospital beds per resident. Supply tends to create demand. This explains the existence of prefectures with a significant national health expenditure that cannot be explained by their age composition.

It will therefore be useful to consider, as a transitional measure, model benefits that take into account the number of hospital beds in a prefecture. An estimation will be attempted here. Regression of the benefit per young subscriber, (B/N^-), with respect to the ratio of elderly subscribers to young subscribers, (N^+/N^-), and the number of hospital beds per person, (F/N^-), produces the following result.

$$B/N^- = 146 + 285N^+/N^- + 1602F/N^- + u$$
$$(7.491)\quad(6.946)\qquad(11.523)$$
$$Adjusted\ R^2 = 0.900$$

The coefficient of determination for this equation is quite high. Multiplying both terms of the equation by N^- gives

$$B = 146N^- + 285N^+ + 1602F + u \cdot N^-$$

In other words, each additional young subscriber would increase annual National Health Insurance benefit payments by 150,000 yen in the prefecture in question, but each additional elderly subscriber would increase benefit payments by 290,000 yen. On the other hand, if the number of hospital beds were to increase, this alone would increase benefit payments by 1.6 million yen per bed.

The theoretical values for National Health Insurance benefit payments for each prefecture obtained in this way represent expected values for benefits corresponding to the current age structure allocation of hospital beds in each prefecture. The amount of model benefits estimated here with consideration of the number of hospital beds will be termed "transitional model benefits."

Let us suppose that the national government provides transitional model benefits to the prefectures in the initial stage of the proposed reforms.

If the amount financed by the national government exceeded the actual benefits paid, the prefecture would again be able to use the surplus at its own discretion; as a result, the greater the inflow of elderly residents, the greater the benefit to the local economy and the greater the improvement in local finances. Because of this, incentives to control inflows of the elderly would disappear.

In this case also, the fact that the prefectures could not influence the amount provided by the national government would give them an incentive to reduce expenses per person.

8 The Process of Transition

Because the allocation of hospital beds is inherently arbitrary, the transitional model benefits system would not produce an efficient mechanism for the choice of living area on the part of health insurance subscribers. Prefectures with an excessive allocation of hospital beds would receive a greater amount of National Health Insurance benefits, and would therefore be able to construct abundant facilities for the elderly. This would mean that the choice of region of residence by the elderly would be dependent upon an arbitrary allocation of hospital beds.

It would therefore be necessary to reallocate the number of hospital beds in Japan's regions to cope with the different demand for medical care in each region. To carry out such a reallocation with minimal political resistance, it would be useful to offer compensation to vested interests in administrative regions to which a large number of hospital beds are currently allocated. One method of doing so would be to allow local governments to trade rights over allocated hospital beds with other local governments. Another possibility would be to uniformly reduce the number of hospital beds allocated to local governments by 10% each year, and reallocate the number of beds that has been reduced to other regions through bidding.[6] By this means, in ten years the entire current allocation of hospital beds would have been retired, and all beds would have been reallocated through bidding. This would reallocate physicians from regions with an excessive number to underpopulated regions, and correct the current provision of excessive health care benefits to regions with too many physicians.[7]

9 Conclusion

The migration of elderly citizens to regional areas represents the most effective use of land from the perspective of the nation as a whole. In addition, because these elderly citizens would bring their pensions with them, such a movement would also benefit local economies. Nevertheless, this is not happening in Japan, because under the current National Health Insurance system an inflow of elderly residents would place a significant burden on the public finances of local governments, a situation that discourages local governments from providing facilities for the elderly. The design of the current National Health Insurance system ensures that local governments will attempt to restrict inflows of elderly residents.

In Japan up to the present, the national government has compelled governments in regional areas to use local tax revenues in order to partially finance even services which should, fundamentally, be entirely financed by the national government. As a result, local governments have been reluctant to accept the elderly, low-income earners, and others who would provide little tax revenue for their areas. National systems artificially push the elderly and low-income earners into large cities, which do not possess a comparative advantage in the provision of services for these residents. Of these national systems, this tendency is particularly marked in the National Health Insurance system.

This chapter has proposed that the national government should provide National Health Insurance model benefits to Japan's prefectures, allowing the prefectures to freely use any surpluses over the amount of benefits actually paid at their own discretion. This reform would eliminate the incentive for local governments to discourage inflows of the elderly, and would offer them an incentive to economize on benefit payments through preventative initiatives.

This chapter has estimated the amount of final model benefits, APMB, based exclusively on the age of National Health Insurance subscribers, in addition to transitional model benefits, which consider the number of hospital beds allocated to the prefecture. It has also proposed measures to enable the transition from the transitional model benefit to the final model benefit.

If the system of regional public finances related to social expenditure for the elderly were reformed in the manner suggested here, and the fiscal burden for the elderly was removed from local governments, local governments in regional areas would approve construction of facilities for the elderly, allowing the inflow of elderly residents with their pensions. Taking advantage of inexpensive land prices, the greatest comparative advantage possessed by regional areas, a new industry of social work would be created in regional areas, contributing to their revitalization. A steady flow of elderly citizens from large cities to regional areas would also create the possibility of a similar movement among young people seeking employment in the area of elderly services.

At present, the Ministry of Health, Labour and Welfare is entirely preoccupied with integrating management of National Health Insurance at the prefectural level, and appears to have no intention of launching reforms of this type. However, the present system is under severe strain.

Similar reforms are also necessary in the areas of education and the welfare system. Viewed from the perspective of growth strategies for Japan as a whole, now, when the government is particularly concerned with the issue of regional revitalization, is precisely the time to push ahead with the reforms proposed in this chapter.

Notes

1. In the present chapter, local governments include both prefectural and municipal administrations.
2. At present, National Health Insurance benefits are being aggregated at the prefectural level. Because the prefectures will still face a burden even when this process is completed, the factors which work to control inflows of elderly residents will still be in effect. In addition, because this system will basically mean government subsidization of the actual cost of treatment, it will not offer prefectures any motivation to economize on benefit payments.
3. At present, benefit payments are being aggregated at the prefectural level. Nevertheless, this still produces a greater incentive for the reduction of benefit payments than would be the case if the government provided the payments en bloc. However, if the focus were returned to the city, town, and village level, the incentive would become stronger.

4. Because students and homemakers are included in the category of subscribers under the age of 65, they cannot be called "workers." At the same time, because people aged 60 and over are also included, they cannot be called "young people" in the normally accepted sense. However, because they are young by comparison with elderly people aged 65 and above, this category will be called "young subscribers."
5. If we were able to use micro data, it would be possible to estimate model benefits for each age group. However, for the present estimation we are making use of macro data only, and therefore divide the population into "the young" and "the elderly."
6. The same result could be achieved by raising the annual rental fee paid to the government by the holders of rights by 10% increments.
7. For concrete measures to be put in place during the transitional phase, see Hatta (2016b).

References

Hatta, Tatsuo (1996), "*Remark*," in Hatta, T. et al. (eds.), Fukushi wa Toushi Dearu (Welfare is an Investment), Nihon Hyoron Sha Press, pp. 172–173.

Hatta, Tatsuo (2015a). '*Chihososei wo Tou (Ge) –Iju no Shouheki-teppai koso Senketsu* (Questioning Regional Revitalization (Part 2): Removing Barriers to Immigration Is the First Priority),' *Nihon Keizai Shimbun*, Morning Edition, February 6, 2015 (in Japanese).

Hatta, Tatsuo (2015b). "*Kokudo no Kinkoaru-hatten' Ron wa Nihon no Suitai wo Maneku* ('Balanced National Development' Threatens Japan with Decline).' *Zenshiten: Jinko-kyugen to Jichitai-shometsu* (The Issues in Question: Rapid Population Decline and the Disappearance of Small Municipalities in Japan), Jiji Press, Ltd., February 2015, pp. 64–67 (in Japanese).

Hatta, Tatsuo (2016a). "*Kokuho no "Moderu-kyuhugaku" Kokkohutanseido' niyoru Chihososei* (Regional Revitalization via a System for the Contribution of "Model Benefits" by the Government),' *Japanese Journal of Health Economics and Policy*, Vol. 27, No. 2, pp. 71–84 (in Japanese).

Hatta, Tatsuo (2016b). '*Koreika to Chihozaisei* (Aging Society and Local Government Finance).' *East Asian Economic Perspectives* (Journal of AGI), December 2016, No.27, Vol.2, pp. 1–14 (http://shiten.agi.or.jp/2016/12/1407/) (in Japanese).

Hayashi, Masayoshi (2012). Channels of stabilization in a system of local public health insurance: the case of the National Health Insurance in Japan. *CIRJE-F-847.*

Hayashi, Masayoshi (2015). 'Health Care, Long-term Care, and Local Public Finances.' *SPACE NIRA*, Unit 01-B.

Iwamoto, Yasushi (1996), "Shian: Iryohokenseido Ichigenka (Designing an Integration of Health Insurance Groups)," *Nihon Keizai Kenkyu (JCER Economic Journal)*, No. 33, November, pp. 119–142 (included in Hatta, T. and Yashiro, N. (eds.) (1998), "*Shakaihoken Kaikaku (Social Insurance Reforms)*," Series Gendai Keizai Kenkyu Vol. 16 (Contemporary Economic Study Series Vol. 16), Nihon Keizai Shimbun) (in Japanese).

Iwamoto, Yasushi (2015). 'Designing New Systems through Risk Adjustment.' *SPACE NIRA*, Unit 01-A.

Kawabuchi, Koichi (2002). *Iryo kaikaku –Itami wo kanjinai seidosekkei wo* (Health Care Reform). Tokyo Keizai Shinposha (in Japanese).

Ministry of Health, Labour and Welfare (2015). 'Documents Prepared by National Health Insurance Division, Health Insurance Bureau, MHLW for "*Zenkoku Koreishairyo Shukannka(bu) cho oyobi Kokuminkenko Hoken Shukanka(bu) cho narabini Koki-koreishairyo Koikirengo Jimukyokucho Kaigi* (National Meetings for Department/Division Chiefs of Elderly Medical Service, Department/ Division Chiefs of National Health Insurance and Secretary-generals of Wide Area Unions for the Late-stage Medical Care System for the Elderly)"' (in Japanese).

Ministry of Land, Infrastructure, Transport and Tourism (2016). *2014 Land Price Research by Prefectural Governments.*

Okabe, Yoji (2014). '*Kino shitenai byoshokisei no zenpai wo –Kitokukenneki wo hogosuru kyousouseigen seisaku* (Abolishing the regulation for the number of hospital beds which failed to function – Competition-restrictive policies protecting vested interests).' *Kinyu Zaisei Business* (Financial & Fiscal Businesss), 10392, pp. 12–17, Jiji Press, Ltd (in Japanese).

Suzuki, Wataru (2010). *Shakaihosho no 'Futsugo na Shinjitu'* ('Inconvenient Truth' of Social Security). Nikkei Publishing Inc (in Japanese).

Suzuki, Wataru (2015). 'Local Government Financing of Health Insurance and Regional Revitalization—Facilitating Migration of the Elderly.' *SPACE NIRA*, Unit 01 Kick-off paper.

PART V

Administrative Reforms: Measures to Address Japan's Low Birthrate

CHAPTER 14

Measures to Address Japan's Low Birth Rate

Tatsuo Hatta

Abstract A well-known Masuda Report, published in 2014, proposed that Japan's birth rate could be increased by encouraging the migration of young people from the Tokyo Metropolitan Area (TMA) to regional areas. The chapters in this section demonstrate that this proposal is based on a misreading of the facts.

Masayuki Nakagawa demonstrates that the birth rate is lower in the inner city than in the suburbs in most major metropolitan areas, and that the birth rates of many regional cities are lower than those of suburban cities in the TMA. Because of this, the migration of young people to regional areas would not increase Japan's fertility rate.

Wataru Suzuki shows that improvement of the system of regional public finances would boost the fertility rate of the nation as a whole.

Keywords Childcare • Fertility rate • Low birth rate • Marriage • Tokyo metropolis

T. Hatta (✉)
Asian Growth Research Institute, Fukuoka, Japan

T. Hatta (ed.), *Economic Challenges Facing Japan's Regional Areas*,
https://doi.org/10.1007/978-981-10-7110-2_14

"Birth rates in Japan differ between regions, and any national measures intended to improve its birth rate have to take this fact into consideration."

Hiroya Masuda and the Japan Policy Council in 2014 made the best-known proposal for improving birth rates following this line of thinking. But its proposal is based on a misreading of the facts.[1]

In Chap. 15, Masayuki Nakagawa (2018) clarifies the factors that resulted in this misreading. In Chap. 16, Wataru Suzuki (2018) proposes the reform of the system of regional public finances as a means of improving the birth rate.

The Masuda Report (2014) argues that because Tokyo's birth rate is low and that of regional areas is high, promoting the migration of young people from Tokyo to regional areas would increase the birth rate in Japan as a whole.

It is true that Tokyo's birth rate is low. However, "moving young people from Tokyo to regional areas" does not constitute an effective measure to address the nation's diminishing birth rate.

Figure 14.1 shows the total fertility rates of government-designated cities and the Tokyo metropolis. As this demonstrates, the Tokyo metropolis's fertility rate is close to the lowest. But the fertility rates of large cities in the Greater Tokyo Area are high when compared with those of large cities in regional areas. Indeed, the fertility rates of Saitama City, Chiba

Fig. 14.1 Total fertility rate in government-designated cities and Tokyo (2010). Source: Ministry of Health, Labour and Welfare, Vital Statistics (2010), Statistics Bureau, Ministry of Internal Affairs and Communications, System of Social and Demographic Statistics

City, Yokohama City, Kawasaki City, and Sagamihara City, which are all in the Greater Tokyo Area, are higher than those of Fukuoka City, Sendai City, or Sapporo City.

Masuda's assertions are therefore based on a fundamental misreading of the actual situation.

Why, then, is the birth rate of the Tokyo metropolis so low? Hatta (2015; 2016, p. 73) and Nakagawa (2015) advance the following explanation: Female students and new female graduates come to Tokyo from regional areas for education and employment. When these women marry and begin to have children, they move to suburban areas such as Chiba and Saitama in search of cheaper rents.[2]

For this reason, the birth rate of the Tokyo metropolis remains low, while the birth rates of the surrounding cities are higher. By contrast, in the case of the majority of other large cities in Japan, the greater part of the suburban area is incorporated within the city itself, and hence birth rates are higher than they are in Tokyo, where the greater part of the suburban area is outside the metropolitan area.

Nakagawa (2015) demonstrates using statistical data that in the case of both the Greater Tokyo Area and the Greater Sendai Area, the rate of marriage is high in suburban areas and low in the central city area. In Chap. 15, Nakagawa (2018) demonstrates that the same phenomenon can be observed in Fukuoka City and Sapporo City. This is to say that the tendency displayed by Tokyo is also displayed by Sendai, Fukuoka, and Sapporo.[3]

Nakagawa (2018) argues that this singular disparity between fertility rates in the Tokyo metropolis and the suburban cities in the Greater Tokyo Area misled Masuda to believe that the Greater Tokyo Area's birth rate is low while the birth rate in regional areas is high. Demonstrating that the birth rate discrepancy between inner city and suburbs is a general phenomenon which is also true of other metropolitan areas, Nakagawa shows that the migration of young people to regional areas would not be an effective measure to respond to Japan's low birth rate.

In Chap. 16, Suzuki (2018) goes on to show that improvement of the system of regional public finances would boost the fertility rate of the nation as a whole.

According to Suzuki, when a city directs public expenditure toward measures designed to shorten waiting lists for childcare, "childcare refugees" surge in from the surrounding cities, which offsets the initial effect of shortening the list. When the number of children requiring childcare in a specific municipality increases, the consequent increase in expenses is not fully covered by government grants, resulting in an increase in net costs for the municipality, discouraging efforts to improve the childrearing environment with the ultimate result that responses cannot be put in place in time. The consequence is that the wait for childcare places continues to be a serious problem in large cities.

Suzuki proposes that the fundamental solution to this problem is for the government to provide "model benefits" for childrearing support measures to each of the nation's municipalities, enabling them to provide support for childrearing without financial burden. In this "model benefit," the government would pay municipalities the full amount necessary for standard childcare services. As a result, municipalities would experience zero burden in implementing standard childrearing support measures, and would be able to provide for the increase in expenses for childrearing support measures due to population influx through increased support from the government, thus eliminating the problem of undersupply.[4]

Suzuki further indicates that the government's subsidies are calculated, and hence increased, two years after any increase in the number of children of childcare age in a given municipality, and that this fact leads to a delay in measures to respond to the issue of children waiting for childcare services. Because of this, the higher the population growth rate of the city is, the more serious the problem of the childcare waiting list becomes.

The adoption of appropriate fiscal measures to address this problem would allow municipalities to develop their childcare facilities as needed, with no concern over an influx of "childcare refugees." All things considered, this could be expected to have a significant effect on efforts to respond to Japan's declining birth rate.

Notes

1. Hatta (2015, 2016), Nakagawa (2015).
2. Hatta (2015) argues that while the birth rate of the Tokyo metropolitan area is low, that of the bed towns in the Greater Tokyo Area is high. Nakagawa (2015) uses statistical data to show differences in the marriage rate by age group between central cities and suburban areas in Japan.
3. In the case of Sapporo, however, the birth rate is low despite the existence of a relatively large greater metropolitan area. Nakagawa (2018) indicates that the reason for this remains unclear.

4. Note that the concept of the central government's provision of "model benefits" for child hearing support is slowly related to that for medical and nursing cares for the aged discussed in Part IV.

References

Hatta, Tatsuo (2015), "*Chihososei wo Tou (Ge) –Iju no Shouheki-teppai koso Senketsu* (Questioning Regional Revitalization (Part 2): Removing Barriers to Immigration Is the First Priority)," *Nihon Keizai Shimbun*, February 6, 2015 (In Japanese).

Hatta, Tatsuo (2016), "*'Kokuho no 'Moderu-kyuhugaku' Kokkohutanseido' niyoru Chihososei* (Regional Revitalization via a System for the Contribution of "Model Benefits" by the Government)," *Japanese Journal of Health Economics and Policy*, Vol. 27, No. 2, pp. 71–84 (In Japanese).

Masuda, Hiroya and The Japan Policy Council (2014), "*Shometsu-kanosei Toshi 896 Zenrisuto no Shogeki: 523 wa Jinko 1-man-nin Ika* (The Impact of the List of 896 Regional Cities that Might Disappear: 523 Have Populations of 10,000 or Less)," *Chuo Koron*, Vol. 129, No. 6, June 2014, pp. 32–43 (In Japanese).

Nakagawa, Masayuki (2015), "*Tokyo wa 'Nihon no Kekkon' ni Koken –Jinkobunsan wa Kajokainyu* (Tokyo Contributes to Marriage in Japan – Decentralization of the Population Would Represent Excessive Intervention)," in *Oiru Toshi, 'Eraberu Rogo' de Sonae wo –Chihososei to Shoshika, Giron wo Wakeyo* (Preparing for Aging Cities by Offering Choices to the Elderly – Towards Separating Discussion of Regional Revitalization and the Low Birth Rate in Japan), Report of the City Study Group, Japan Center for Economic Research, July, 2015, pp. 45–59 (In Japanese).

Nakagawa, Masayuki (2018), "Marriage and Childcare in the Metropolitan Areas: A Comparison of Sapporo City and the Greater Fukuoka Area," in T. Hatta (ed.), *Economic Challenges Facing Japan's Regional Areas*, Plagrave Macmillan, pp. 137–143.

Suzuki, Wataru (2018), "Childcare and Measures Targeting Japan's Low Birth Rate: What Effect Can the Decentralization of Authority Have on the Birth Rate?" in T. Hatta (ed.), *Economic Challenges Facing Japan's Regional Areas*, Plagrave Macmillan, pp. 145–154.

CHAPTER 15

Marriage and Childcare in the Metropolitan Areas: A Comparison of Sapporo City and the Greater Fukuoka Area

Masayuki Nakagawa

Abstract This chapter shows that the tendency for the rate of marriage to be low in central cities and high in outlying cities is due to the fact that central cities function as a sphere for couple formation, while outlying cities represent the venue for life following couple formation. However, while it is generally the case that the marriage rate in outlying cities offsets the marriage rate in the central city so that the marriage rate in the greater metropolitan area becomes almost identical to that of the region as a whole, the Greater Sapporo Area is an exception to this rule. This chapter suggests that one reason for this anomaly is the existence of a central city which is too large as a result of amalgamations.

Keywords Birth rate • Sphere for couple formation • Central city • Outlying city • Fiscal externality

M. Nakagawa (✉)
Graduate School of Economics, Nihon University, Tokyo, Japan

T. Hatta (ed.), *Economic Challenges Facing Japan's Regional Areas*,
https://doi.org/10.1007/978-981-10-7110-2_15

1 Introduction

A report published by the Japan Policy Council in 2014 argued that the concentration of Japan's population in Tokyo, a city with a low birth rate, was lowering the birth rate in the nation as a whole, and that it would therefore be necessary to correct the concentration of the population in the Tokyo area. However, Tokyo's low birth rate originates in a low rate of marriage. Nakagawa (2015) argues that Tokyo, the central city of the Greater Tokyo Area, functions as an effective market for the matching of males and females to form couples, and that couples that form in Tokyo then move to outlying cities in neighboring prefectures where the cost of living is lower. Considered from the perspective of the Greater Tokyo Area, incorporating the three surrounding prefectures, the problem of the birth rate is therefore not so severe.[1]

A comparison of the percentage of unmarried women aged 25–49 in Japan's government-designated cities and the 23 special wards of Tokyo with the national average shows that the percentage is higher in almost all of the cities regarded as the central cities of major metropolitan areas. The percentage is particularly high, at 7–8%, in Sapporo City, the 23 special wards of Tokyo, Kyoto City, Osaka City, and Fukuoka City. However, the discrepancy between the national average and figures for urban areas declines significantly if we focus on major metropolitan areas that straddle prefectural boundaries, such as the Greater Tokyo Area and the Greater Osaka Area. The same is even true of Sapporo City and Fukuoka City, metropolitan areas which do not exceed prefectural boundaries.

2 Marriage Rate in Sapporo City and Fukuoka City

The percentage of married women in the 25–49 age group (the number of women in this age group with spouses divided by the total number of women in the age group) is 55.9% for the entire nation; the figure is lower in Sapporo City (51.2%) and in Fukuoka City (47.8%). Looking at prefectural units, the figures are only slightly lower than the national average, with Hokkaido Prefecture at 54.2% and Fukuoka Prefecture at 52%. Figure 15.1 compares marriage rates in Sapporo City, the central city of the Greater Sapporo Area, the outlying cities in the Greater Sapporo Area, and the Greater Sapporo Area itself with the prefectural average;[2] Fig. 15.2 compares marriage rates in Fukuoka City, the outlying cities in the Greater Fukuoka Area, and the Greater Fukuoka Area with the prefectural average.[3]

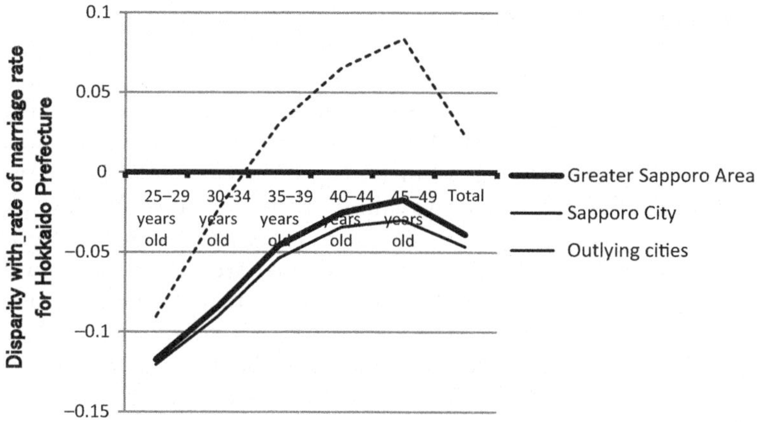

Fig. 15.1 Disparity in rate of marriage for women aged 25–49 between Greater Sapporo Area and Hokkaido Prefecture. Source: Formulated using data from 2010 National Census (Ministry of Internal Affairs and Communications)

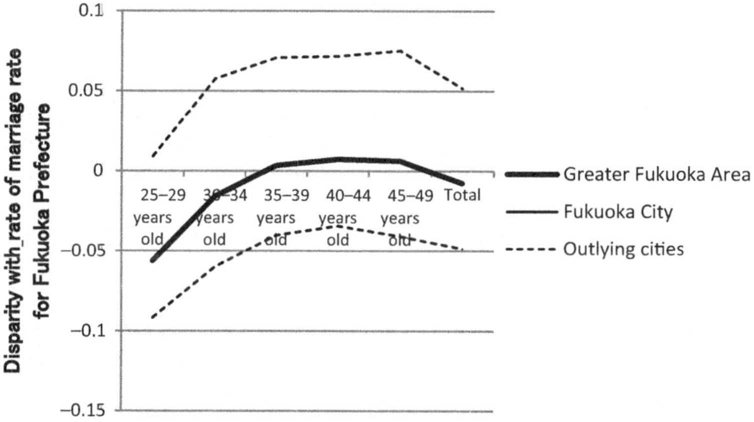

Fig. 15.2 Disparity in rate of marriage for women aged 25–49 between Greater Fukuoka Area and Fukuoka Prefecture. Source: Formulated using data from 2010 National Census (Ministry of Internal Affairs and Communications)

The marriage rate among women in the younger age groups for Sapporo City is around 10% lower than the rate for the prefecture, and the rate for the city is lower than the rate for the prefecture in all age groups. The rate of marriage among the 35 and above age groups in the outlying cities of the Greater Sapporo Area significantly exceeds the rate for the prefecture. However, the rate of marriage for the Greater Sapporo Area as a whole in this age group displays almost exactly the same tendency as the marriage rate for Sapporo City, and is around 4% lower than the prefectural rate. As in the case of the Greater Sapporo Area, the figure for outlying cities in the Greater Fukuoka Area is higher than the prefectural rate. However, the rate for the Greater Fukuoka Area is significantly boosted by the rate for the outlying cities, with the result that the rate for the metropolitan area as a whole is almost exactly the same as the rate for the prefecture.

3 Existence of Enormous Central Cities

Differences in city structure affect this difference in the marriage rate. Comparing the percentage of the population of the entire greater metropolitan area residing in the central city, we find a figure of 81.7% for the Greater Sapporo Area, but only 59% for the Greater Fukuoka Area.

This is a result of the enormous size of Sapporo City. The area of the Greater Fukuoka Area is 1282.99 square kilometers, and Fukuoka City represents only 27% of this area at 343.39 km^2. By contrast, at 1121.26 km^2, the area of Sapporo City is almost equivalent to that of the entire Greater Fukuoka Area.

The potential range of residence for individuals who commute to the central business district of a major metropolitan area and enjoy the benefits of an agglomeration economy has fixed spatial limits. The area of the Greater Sapporo Area is extremely large (3205.12 km^2), but the majority of its population resides in the central city. This suggests the possibility that by contrast with the Greater Fukuoka Area, where couples which have formed in Fukuoka City are able to choose an environment in which to raise their children from among a diverse range of outlying cities, the choice for couples which have formed in Sapporo City is limited to the central city itself.

There is a considerable difference between the childrearing environment that can be provided by a single local government and that provided by multiple local governments. The author calculated the ratio between cost of living and salary for the wards making up Sapporo City and the wards and municipalities making up the Greater Fukuoka Area. The average cost of residential land by municipality in the 2014 Land Price Research by Prefectural Governments was used for cost of living. Taxable income divided by the number of taxpayers, from the Ministry of Internal Affairs and Communications' Survey of Municipal Taxes (1975–2013), was used for income.

Figure 15.3 shows results for cost of living divided by income for each ward and municipality, ordered from lowest to highest, against the cumulative percentage of the population of Sapporo City and the Fukuoka City employment area corresponding to each level of cost of living/income. The results for Sapporo City are distributed between a minimum of 0.014 and a maximum of 0.038, while the results for the Greater Fukuoka Area are distributed between a minimum of 0.007, half the minimum for Sapporo City, and a maximum of 0.053. Couples in the Greater Fukuoka Area have a wide

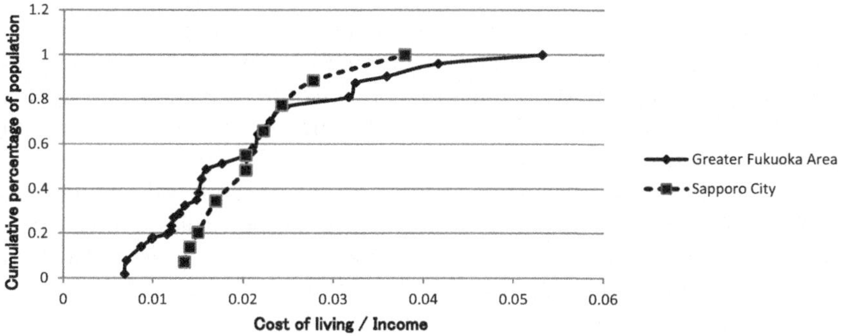

Fig. 15.3 Comparison of ratio between cost of living and income for Sapporo City and the Greater Fukuoka Area (2013). Source: Formulated using data from the 2014 Land Price Research by Prefectural Governments and the Survey of Municipal Taxes (1975–2013) (Ministry of Internal Affairs and Communications). The data for "the average cost of residential land by municipality" in 2013 can be obtained at the website Land and Property in Japan of Land Economy and Construction Industries Bureau, MLIT, from "Table 15" (in Japanese) (http://tochi.mlit.go.jp/chika/kouji/2014/xls/29.xls), and the data for "taxable income" and "the number of taxpayers" in 2013 can be obtained at Demographic and Economic Data by Municipalities of Cabinet Office's website from "Taxable Income" (in Japanese) (http://www5.cao.go.jp/keizai-shimon/kaigi/special/future/keizai-jinkou_data/file09.xls) and "The number of taxpayers" (in Japanese)" (http://www5.cao.go.jp/keizai-shimon/kaigi/special/future/keizai-jinkou_data/file10.xls)

range of choice in terms of their living environment, including residential areas in which the cost of living is extremely low, while couples in Sapporo City have only a comparatively limited range of choice.

4 Conclusion

Why do young people cluster in cities? Two factors will be focused on here.

(1) Diverse, high-productivity companies exploiting the benefits of an agglomeration economy are concentrated in cities, with a consequent concentration of employment opportunities.
(2) An environment promoting face-to-face communication and the existence of a diverse range of single people make the city a marriage market that matches individuals effectively.

Factors 1 and 2 overlap in attracting young people to the city, but in the case of Japan, where there is limited migration for employment, in many cases restrictions on the choice of employer prior to the formation of a couple determines the choice of residential area following marriage. In order for both factors to function adequately, it is essential that the metropolitan area is made up of a central city in which young people are able to work and earn a living, and outlying cities in which they are able to live cheaply. Unless both of these factors function, young people who have moved to the city due to factor 1, and young people who have moved due to factor 2 but have not been able to marry, will remain in the central city without marrying.

Outlying cities are able to take a free ride on the ample employment opportunities, municipal services, and public services such as public transport networks and art galleries that exist in the central city. If the existence of these cities gives rise to fiscal externalities, it is also possible that it creates the potential for married life for young people in the greater metropolitan area. Sapporo City took its present form as a result of massive municipal amalgamations at the time of the 1972 Winter Olympics. It is possible that this is why the city is not adequately provided with outlying cities that offer low-cost living environments within a geographical radius enabling commuting.

The above argument has shown that the tendency for the rate of marriage to be low in the central city because it functions as a sphere for couple formation, and for the rate of marriage to be high in outlying cities because they represent the venue for life after couple formation, is generally applicable to metropolitan areas. However, while it is generally the case that the marriage rate in the outlying cities offsets the marriage rate in the central city so that the marriage rate in the greater metropolitan area becomes almost identical to that of the region as a whole, the Greater Sapporo Area is an exception to this rule. This chapter has suggested the existence of a central city which is too large as a result of amalgamations as a factor in this, but it is to be hoped that further research will elucidate other factors which are specific to Sapporo City.

Notes

1. The same explanation was previously proposed by Hatta (2015). Nakagawa (2015) also indicates that the same tendency can be observed in the Greater Sendai Area.
2. The Sapporo-Otaru urban employment area is used (see http://www.csis.u-tokyo.ac.jp/UEA/ for a definition of "urban employment area"). This urban employment area consists of seven suburban cities and towns, including Ebetsu City, with Sapporo and Otaru as the central cities. In order to simplify the discussion in the present chapter, Otaru is considered as representing one of the suburban cities.
3. The Fukuoka urban employment area is used. This urban employment area consists of 18 suburban cities and towns, including Ogori City, with Fukuoka City as the central city.

References

Hatta, Tatsuo (2015), "*Chihososei wo Tou (Ge) –Iju no Shouheki-teppai koso Senketsu* (Questioning Regional Revitalization (Part 2): Removing Barriers to Immigration is the First Priority)," *Nihon Keizai Shimbun*, February 6, 2015 (in Japanese).

Nakagawa, Masayuki (2015), "*Tokyo wa 'Nihon no Kekkon' ni Koken –Jinkobunsan wa Kajokainyu* (Tokyo Contributes to Marriage in Japan—Decentralization of the Population Would Represent Excessive Intervention)," in *Oiru Toshi, 'Eraberu Rogo' de Sonae wo –Chihososei to Shoshika, Giron wo Wakeyo* (Preparing for Aging Cities by Offering Choices to the Elderly—Towards Separating Discussion of Regional Revitalization and the Low Birth Rate in Japan), Report of the City Study Group, Japan Center for Economic Research, July 2015, pp. 45–59 (in Japanese).

CHAPTER 16

Childcare and Measures Targeting Japan's Low Birth Rate: What Effect Can the Decentralization of Authority Have on the Birth Rate?

Wataru Suzuki

Abstract The belief exists that the concentration of Japan's population in Tokyo is responsible for the nation's low birth rate, and that this issue should therefore be addressed by means of regional revitalization. This belief is based on a misreading of the facts. It will be essential to put into effect measures targeting the low birth rate in the cities where the population is concentrated. We identify two reasons for the failure of measures targeting the low birth rate to make progress in Japan's major cities: (1) a time lag between population influxes and the provision of public funding for childcare, and (2) the fact that surrounding municipalities are able to enjoy a free ride on a specific municipality's expenditure on childcare due to a spillover effect.

Keywords Regional revitalization • Childrearing support measures • Low birth rate • Spillover effect • Waiting list problem • Model benefit • Voucher

W. Suzuki (✉)
Faulty of Economics, Gakushuin University, Tokyo, Japan

T. Hatta (ed.), *Economic Challenges Facing Japan's Regional Areas*,
https://doi.org/10.1007/978-981-10-7110-2_16

1 Ensuring Employment Opportunities Is Essential for Measures Addressing the Declining Birth Rate

The important thing to bear in mind when considering the appropriate direction for measures targeting Japan's low birth rate and the nation's regional revitalization initiatives is that measures targeting the birth rate implemented by local municipalities cannot, in isolation, boost the declining birth rate or arrest the declining population in Japan's regional areas.

From an economic perspective, the choice on the part of a married couple to have children can be considered a type of joint investment in a consumer durable. However, this consumer durable is a private good that cannot be bought or sold, and one for which the utility of consumption (the joy of raising a child) is available only to that couple. Childrearing entails considerable cost over an extended period, and, particularly in Japan, it is normal for the wife to stop working and devote herself exclusively to the task. If, during the period of childrearing when the wife's income is interrupted, there are fears regarding the possibility of the husband losing his job, or a significant risk of the breakdown of the marriage due to economic problems, a "hold-up problem" can arise. Such fears that the carpet may be pulled out from under a couple make the initial decision to have children a difficult one. In Japan, where marriage and children are often considered inextricably linked, this can result in indecision with regard to getting married at all.

From this perspective, what is essential for strategies to genuinely respond to Japan's low birth rate is not merely measures to support childrearing (provision of childcare, etc.), but also the guarantee of employment opportunities for married couples, allowing them to be confident in their ability to maintain a stable married life over the long term.

2 Concentration on City-based Measures is the Practical Approach

The Masuda Report published in 2014 by the Japan Policy Council (Japan Policy Council, 2014) had a considerable impact on Japanese society due to its claim that the outflow of population from Japan's regional areas to large cities would increase, and that as many as half of the nation's small municipalities were at risk of disappearing. However, from an economic perspective, there are problems with the report's judgment that the concentration of population in Tokyo and the flow of population to major cities is promoting an accelerating decline in the birth rate in Japan as a whole, and its insistence that it will be necessary to halt this movement of the population in order to address the issue of the nation's low birth rate.

As Hatta (2015a, b) makes clear, the preconceptions behind the Masuda Report—that the nation's population is excessively concentrated in Tokyo, and that the birth rate in the Greater Tokyo Area is lower than the birth rate in the nation's regional areas—are both factual errors. Therefore, even if we ensure that young people stay in regional areas from which employment opportunities are disappearing, or promote migration from large cities, the birth rate will not improve.

It is natural that young people will move from regional areas marked by declining populations and economic decline to large cities in search of employment opportunities. Because the concentration of population in major cities such as Greater Tokyo and the government-designated cities creates an agglomeration advantage, it is desirable as a growth strategy for the nation as a whole. Regional revitalization measures, such as diverting city tax revenues to regional areas or unreasonably attempting to halt the flow of population towards big cities, run counter to this natural economic principle. Not only would these measures not function as growth strategies, but they can also be considered as having little effect as measures to address the problem of the low birth rate.[1]

Assuming that the flow of population to large cities is allowed to continue unimpeded, if measures to address the birth rate issue are necessary from a policy perspective, it would be considerably more practical to concentrate resources on measures put into effect in the cities. Naturally, if couples who move to the city desire a limited number of children, and a low birth rate results from their rational choice, excessive policy intervention would not be justified. However, if policies in the cities create obstacles that prevent couples from having their desired number of children, it would be necessary to correct this situation.

3 The Provision of Measures to Support Childrearing Is Lagging Behind Urban Population Increase

For example, in cities with a high degree of population influx, the provision of standard childrearing support measures is failing to keep pace with the continuously increasing population, and it is possible that this is resulting in a reduced birth rate.[2] Figure 16.1 represents the relationship between the total fertility rate and the rate of population increase for government-designated cities and the Tokyo metropolitan area (the area covered by the 23 wards of Tokyo). Figure 16.1 shows a clear negative relationship between the two (coefficient of correlation: −0.38).

In other words, even in an individual city, the birth rate will decline as the rate of population increase becomes higher due to ongoing population influx. One reason for this is that the resources necessary for childrearing support measures do not keep pace with the population increase. From the policy perspective, there is scope for the realization of improvement in this area, and in fact measures implemented here could be expected to be effective in addressing the low birth rate.[3] For example, national tax grants to local governments are calculated based on the situation two years

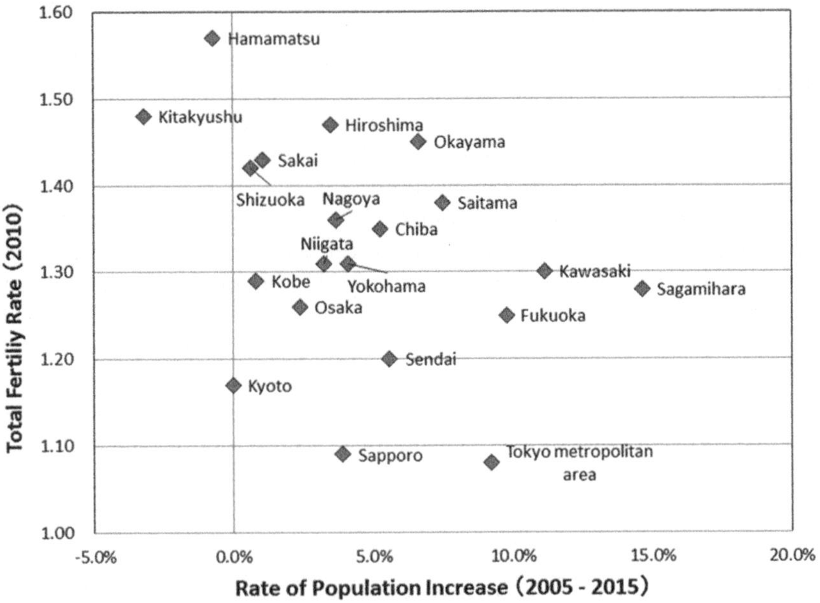

Fig. 16.1 Relationship between total fertility rate and rate of population increase in government-designated cities and the Tokyo metropolitan area. Source: Ministry of Health, Labour and Welfare, Vital Statistics (2010), Ministry of Internal Affairs and Communications, National Census (Various years)

previously. If a projected figure for the grant amount in the area of childrearing support were calculated for the present fiscal year, it would be possible to avoid any lag in the securing of fiscal resources for childrearing support.

4 Externalities of Measures to Respond to Childcare Waiting Lists

In addition, because childrearing support measures in cities with growing populations have externalities, measures in each municipality are undersupplied. For example, the problem of the waiting list for nursery schools is becoming severe in the Tokyo metropolitan area and government-designated cities. If a municipality were to actively institute measures to alleviate the problem while measures were not being advanced in other municipalities, then the surrounding municipalities might enjoy a free ride, and this is one factor that can be pointed to as lying behind this problem.

In the event that municipalities construct new licensed nursery schools, they are left with enormous financial burdens for operating expenses and other costs.[4] The construction of a new licensed nursery school will immediately attract an influx of families raising children from surrounding municipalities in which the waiting list problem is severe, and the municipality will find itself back at square one, despite its expenditure of public funds on new construction. Given this, municipalities adopt a passive stance in relation to measures to address the wait for nursery schools, because they seek to take a free ride (or they do not wish to attract free riders). The same structural problems can be considered to affect childrearing support measures other than measures targeting the waiting list problem, fiscal expenditure on compulsory elementary and junior high school education, and after-school care.

Because of this, many municipalities give low scores to families moving from other municipalities in deciding on applications for entry to licensed nursery schools, offering preferential treatment to applicants who are longer-term residents of their own municipality. There are also examples, such as Setagaya Ward and Suginami Ward in Tokyo, of municipalities which, despite the severity of the waiting list problem, independently establish additional standards far in advance of the minimum government standards for licensed nursery schools (standards for facility area and standards for nursery school teachers), and offer preferential treatment to residents, who inherently possess easier access to licensed nursery schools (Suzuki 2014). Because of the severity of the waiting list problem, the excessive independent measures for the reduction and mitigation of childcare fees implemented by many municipalities in Tokyo also make it difficult for families raising children to move from other municipalities.

Some municipalities, such as Tokyo's Koto Ward, are also limiting the construction of new apartment complexes, in an attempt to prevent an influx of population which would increase childcare and education costs. These distortions of the system interfere with the freedom of individuals to choose where they live. In the sense that they impede the agglomeration advantage, they are also examples of misplaced priorities from the perspective of growth strategy. The following measures can be considered as means of correcting these systemic distortions.

5 Towards the Introduction of "Model Benefits" for Childrearing

The first method would be the implementation of coordination across a wide area, straddling multiple municipalities. For example, because the wards of Yokohama City, unlike Tokyo's wards, are only administrative districts, they are unable to use their own discretion in relation to childcare measures. Because of this, if the Yokohama City mayor, at the top of the city administration, makes the appropriate decision, it is possible to introduce measures to upgrade and expand childcare across all the city's wards. This is a type of coordination of measures across a wide area, and it avoids the problem of externalities that arises when wards are able to act independently and at their own discretion. Yokohama City is famous for having reduced the number of children waiting to enter childcare to zero in 2013 under the leadership of Mayor Fumiko Hayashi, after recording the worst figures in the country in 2010. It can be considered that the ability to roll out measures across a wide area, not possible in Tokyo, lies behind this success.

The second method of correcting systemic distortion would be to introduce a method similar to the *jushochi tokurei* system applied in nursing care insurance to childcare support measures.[5] Specifically, this would mean a system whereby expenses for the provision of childrearing support in the municipality to which a family moves would be borne by the municipality from which the family has moved. This would make free riding impossible, and all municipalities would therefore implement childrearing support measures without hesitation. There would also be no lag in resources provision. However, using this method, it would be difficult to compel municipalities to bear the burden of subsidizing the construction of childcare facilities in addition to their operating expenses. In addition, complex adjustment of the system would be necessary in responding to households for which moving would be troublesome, for example due to the necessity for job relocation.

The third and most radical method would be to establish a system in which the government pays a "model benefit" for childcare support to each municipality, as proposed by Hatta (2015b) as a reform of the National Health Insurance system. This would entail the government providing to municipalities the full basic necessary amount (i.e., the model benefit) for the minimum standard of childcare and education that should be guaranteed by the government. The expense of establishing facilities, in addition to facility operating expenses, would be calculated in the model benefit for each child, and provided to the municipality. Because this method would reduce the burden on municipalities for standard childcare measures to zero, it would enable the problem of insufficient supply to be avoided. It would be possible to provide an amount estimated to ensure that there were no lag in resources, and adjust any excess or shortfall the following year.

Naturally, there would be an additional burden of expense on municipalities which sought to implement measures in excess of the basic standard. But in the case of municipalities making up cities, for which the influx of population would produce economies of scale enabling childcare support measures to be provided more cheaply than the standard amount, a fiscal surplus would be produced, and the amount of the surplus could be invested in further measures.

6 The Issuing of Vouchers Would Also Be an Effective Measure

It would also be possible to provide such model benefits directly to households raising children, as government vouchers for operating expenses and facility upkeep, bypassing the municipality. Because these subsidies would be carried with the childrearing households, municipalities would not obstruct the movement of households; municipalities in urban areas which were able to tailor low-cost childrearing support measures through economies of scale would actually welcome an influx of childrearing households. The use of vouchers would spark competition between licensed childcare facilities, and between licensed and unlicensed childcare facilities. Market principles would increase the supply of childcare and correct the problem of disparities in subsidies between childrearing households, making this a measure that would radically reform the childcare industry as a whole.

In fact, there has been considerable progress over the last ten years in the transfer of funds for childrearing support measures, including childcare, to regional municipalities via the local allocation tax. However, with no significant improvement in the waiting lists for childcare in cities, municipalities in urban areas experiencing an influx of population can be considered to have faced two problems: (1) the inability of childrearing support measures to keep pace with population increase, due to factors including a lag in the provision of government subsidies; and (2) a tendency towards undersupply, due to the effect of externalities on childrearing support measures. Addressing these issues via methods such as the introduction of a model benefits system is the appropriate direction for the decentralization of government authority and measures targeting Japan's low birth rate. Rather than implementing measures with unknown outcomes, we should begin by correcting the distortions in the system.

Notes

1. As already indicated, the choice to have children is initially made possible by an expectation on the part of the parents of long-term employment opportunities and lifestyle stability. The short-term distribution of tax revenues to regional areas will not readily change this situation. In addition, as the author has previously argued in detail (Hatta 2015a, b), whether improvement of the birth rate actually functions as a growth strategy is open to question. There is scope for discussion regarding whether the improvement of the birth rate is appropriate as a policy target.
2. To take an example, in relation to the childcare measures implemented by regional municipalities, because market failures are occurring in the market for female labor, a certain degree of investment of public funds can be justified (Hatta 2008, p. 326). Because it is known that externalities occur in the area of preschool education, a certain degree of investment of public funds is rational. Given this, the implementation by municipalities of standard

basic childrearing support measures and measures to address the low birth rate can be justified economically.

3. This is to say that if the standard of the childrearing support measures implemented by cities of this type had been equivalent to that of other municipalities, the birth rate would have been higher. If policy obstacles result in couples producing fewer than their desired number of children, the correction of these policies would generate immediate results. Of course, it is also possible that other factors result in low birth rates in municipalities with a high rate of population influx, for example the higher cost of land and the lower amount of living space per household. In this case, there would be little scope to increase the birth rate by means of improvements in childrearing support measures.
4. For example, Itabashi Ward, an average municipality in the Tokyo metropolitan area, shoulders 74.2% of the burden of operating expenses for licensed childcare facilities. Parents cover 10.6%, the government funds 8.3%, the city funds 4.1%, and 2.7% is sourced elsewhere (Financial statements for FY 2014: Ratio of financial burden on parents). Theoretically, the government should provide half of the unit cost of childcare, and the city or prefecture a quarter. In practice, a variety of other expenses arise that must be covered by public expenditure, including supplementation of personnel costs for public childcare workers, the municipality's own reduction of childcare fees, and childcare fees for defaulters, with the result that 70–80% of operating expenses are covered by the municipality itself.
5. In the case of an insurance subscriber who moves from their original municipality to another because of a lack of special aged-care homes, the individual's expenses are paid by the nursing care insurance in the original municipality, and the individual pays insurance premiums to the original municipality. The same system is accepted in many nursing care facilities other than special aged-care homes.

References

Hatta, Tatsuo (2008), *Mikuro Keizaigaku 1: Shijo no Shippai to Seihu no Shippai eno Taisaku* (Microeconomics I: Responses to Market Failures and Government Failures), Toyo Keizai Shimposha (In Japanese).

Hatta, Tatsuo (2015a), "*Chihososei wo Tou (Ge) –Iju no Shouheki-teppai koso Senketsu* (Questioning Regional Revitalization (Part 2): Removing Barriers to Immigration Is the First Priority)," *Nihon Keizai Shimbun*, February 6, 2015 (In Japanese).

Hatta, Tatsuo (2015b), "*'Kokuho no 'Moderu-kyuhugaku' Kokkohutanseido' niyoru Chihososei* (Regional Revitalization via a System for the Contribution of "Model

Benefits" by the Government)," *Japanese Journal of Health Economics and Policy*, Vol. 27, No. 2, pp.71–84 (In Japanese).
Japan Policy Council (2014), *Sutoppu shoshika / chiho genki senryaku* (Strategies for Boosting Japan's Birth Rate and Reviving its Regions), May 8, 2014 (www.policycouncil.jp/pdf/prop03/prop03.pdf) (In Japanese).
Suzuki, Wataru (2014), *Shakaihosho Bokoku Ron* (The Collapse of Social Security), Kodansha Shinsho (In Japanese).

PART VI

Administrative Reforms: Local Government Fiscal System

CHAPTER 17

Good and Bad Fiscal Decentralization

Motohiro Sato

Abstract Japan's system of centralized public finance is changing. The independence and responsibility of local governments are increasing. What remains lacking is "marginal fiscal responsibility," which would see local residents bearing the costs of policies decided on by local governments themselves. The short chapters presented here deal with the status and problems of Japan's system of fiscal transfers and property tax reform based on the principle of levying a benefit tax on local residents. The two essential factors for good fiscal decentralization are reform of the existing local allocation tax grants and reorganization of the local tax system. These reforms would ensure the fiscal responsibility of local residents and enhance efficiency. This would also contribute to fiscal reconstruction at the national level.

Keywords Fiscal decentralization • Marginal fiscal responsibility • Local allocation tax • The guarantee of fiscal resources • Property tax • Benefit principle • Local residents • Local governments • Fiscal consolidation • Cost awareness

M. Sato (✉)
Graduate School of Economics, Applied Economics,
School of International and Public Policy, Hitotsubashi University, Tokyo, Japan

T. Hatta (ed.), *Economic Challenges Facing Japan's Regional Areas*,
https://doi.org/10.1007/978-981-10-7110-2_17

Japan's centralized public finance is changing. As indicated by the designation "administrative decentralization system," local governments have previously functioned as little more than subsidiary organizations of the central government, implementing policies and projects formulated by, and for which financial resources are funded by (the guarantee of fiscal resources), the central government. However, the independence and responsibility of local governments is now increasing as a result of a number of factors. These include: (1) the enactment of the Comprehensive Decentralization Act, which, among other things, abolished the imposition of administrative functions on local governments by the national government, in April 2000; (2) the "Great Heisei Mergers" of municipalities, which has roughly halved the number of municipalities in the nation; (3) the "Trinity Reforms," which transferred sources of tax revenue amounting to some trillions of yen from the national government to local governments; and (4) "regional sovereignty reform" under the Democratic Party of Japan (DPJ), among the effects of which was to transform grants to local governments into lump sum payments. Numerous local governments are leading the way in putting administrative and fiscal reforms into effect, including public accounting reform and the evaluation of administrative procedures and projects.

However, the character of the system within which local public finance is organized remains unchanged. A number of points can be made in relation to this fact. (1) The guarantee of fiscal resources for local public finance plans, and the system of local allocation tax grants that actualize this guarantee, are subsidies predicated on the "administrative decentralization system" in which local governments implement policies (the expenditure allocated to local public finance plans) formulated by the national government. (2) Despite the system of local allocation tax grants, local governments are not displaying sufficient autonomy or creativity. Tax grants targeting regional revitalization seek to support advanced local government initiatives, but the decision as to which initiatives are advanced relies heavily on the judgment of the national government. This may induce local governments to create plans that look towards the central government's will rather than utilizing their own creativity and originality. (3) The central government's guarantee of fiscal resources also extends to local debt (municipal debt-covering bonds and bonds which the government has agreed to finance). This implicit credit guarantee has reduced the cost of issuing municipal bonds (interest) to a level similar to that of government bonds. This has been indicated as a factor impeding the more widespread use of Private and Public Partnership/Private Finance Initiative

(PPP/PFI) initiatives, the purpose of which is to make use of private sector funds and management expertise in the upgrading and operation of public facilities. The low interest rate on local government bonds renders the actual cost of public projects and public facilities (including risk) unclear. In addition, it can be seen to have adverse effects on independent municipal policy. The *furusato nozei* ("hometown tax") is a competitive quid pro quo system in which municipalities send local products to taxpayers (donors) as expression of gratitude. Municipalities, mainly the financially well-off municipalities in the nation's urban areas, are also waiving children's medical fees and other costs. An element of excess competition to provide benefits can be found in these measures.

What is lacking in both the guarantee of fiscal resources and the initiatives of local governments is fiscal responsibility on the part of local residents. "Fiscal responsibility" here does not refer to the abolition of subsidies and a requirement for local governments to undertake fiscal management using only their own resources. It is rather a "marginal fiscal responsibility" in which local residents bear the costs of policies and projects (own projects, etc.) decided on by local governments themselves so as to make local residents cost conscious. This type of marginal fiscal responsibility is lacking in current decentralization measures. Taking the consolidation of public facilities as an example, decisions are not being made regarding the maintenance or scrapping of an existing public facility after ensuring that residents understand the additional tax burden that this would entail. For example, the Management Plans for Public Facilities being drawn up by municipalities at present include measures for the consolidation of public facilities. However, there is strong resistance among local residents to the closure or reduction in scale of facilities that benefit them without their having to shoulder any financial burden.

At the same time, disparities between municipalities are also a concern. Under a decentralized system, it would be the role of local allocation tax grants to even out disparities that are not based on the efforts towards self-assistance of the municipality concerned. However, the current system of allocation tax grants has actually weakened fiscal discipline in municipalities and promoted a sense of dependence. Local governments demand their allocation tax grant in all situations. If allocation tax grants are offered before reform efforts are launched, it is doubtful that the reforms will proceed (all the more so if no difficulties in management occur in cases where reforms are not implemented). There are numerous faults in the local taxes that are levied on residents. The exercise of local tax autonomy is weighted too heavily towards corporate taxes (corporate enterprise tax and corporate inhabitant tax). The benefit principle is indicated as the grounds for this, but in practice municipalities are reluctant to levy benefit taxes, including individual inhabitant tax, on residents. Ultimately, taxes are extracted where it is easiest to do so. From a textbook perspective, we are far from the levying of true benefit taxes; for example, even as regards property tax, pointed to as "a good local tax," relief measures exist for small-scale residences that reduce the tax standard by five-sixths.

Ultimately, the point of divergence between good fiscal decentralization and bad fiscal decentralization is the fiscal responsibility (cost awareness) of residents. When we talk about fiscal decentralization, the structure of confrontation between the national and local governments is sharply highlighted, but what is really at issue is the relationship between local governments and residents. How can we realize fiscal management that considers this relationship? Local residents who lack cost awareness have no interest in municipal fiscal management. As a result, they do not monitor fiscal management, and fiscal discipline becomes lax. The two essential factors for good fiscal decentralization are: (1) reform of the existing local allocation tax grants; and (2) reorganization of the local tax system. The short chapters in this section deal with the status and issues of Japan's system of fiscal transfers (factor 1) and property tax reform based on the principle of levying a benefit tax on local residents (factor 2). In Chap. 18, Professor Wataru Kobayashi considers the scope and the level of the guarantee of fiscal resources, the measurement of the fiscal capability of a municipality, and the treatment of municipalities that do not receive the grants as three issues related to local allocation tax grants. In Chap. 19, Professor Tomomi Miyazaki looks at the reasons the property tax does not satisfy the benefit principle (the limits on local tax autonomy, the existence of a variety of preferential measures, and the possibility that the existing property tax is de facto a capital tax), and proposes reforms which will make the property tax a benefit tax. Naturally, while we may talk about "local governments" in general terms, there is a tremendous range among them in terms of fiscal and economic capability. Local governments also differ in terms of their capacity for independence and fiscal responsibility. In the sense that the same administrative duties and the same extent of autonomy have been applied to all local governments, Japan's initiatives towards fiscal decentralization have been "centralized" or uniform. If it were possible to classify local governments into a number of groups based on factors including fiscal capability, fiscal transfers could be conducted and the local tax system (the allocation of tax revenue sources) could be organized based on these groups.

The government is currently seeking to achieve fiscal consolidation, balancing the primary fiscal balance by FY 2020, and is advancing Integrated Economic and Fiscal Reforms (the Plan to Advance Economic and Fiscal Revitalization) as part of its efforts. The realization of increased efficiency in local expenditure (including measures such as PPP/PFI, use of information technology in daily operations, and wide area administration) is positioned as an important axis of these measures. If fiscal decentralization stimulates cost awareness in local residents, resulting in a greater level of interest in and monitoring of the municipal administration, efficient fiscal management at the micro level (the level of each municipality) will be enhanced, which may in turn contribute to fiscal reconstruction at the macro level (the national or regional level) as well.

References

Miyazaki, Tomomi (2018), "Decentralization Reform and Property Tax in Japan: A Consideration of the Benefit Principle," in T. Hatta (ed.), *Economic Challenges Facing Japan's Regional Areas*, Plagrave Macmillan, pp. 173–179.

Kobayashi, Wataru (2018), "Examining Functions of Intergovernmental Fiscal Transfer," in T. Hatta (ed.), *Economic Challenges Facing Japan's Regional Areas*, Plagrave Macmillan, pp. 163–171.

CHAPTER 18

Examining Functions of Intergovernmental Fiscal Transfer

Wataru Kobayashi

Abstract This chapter considers three issues in relation to the two functions of Japan's local allocation tax grants—the function of guaranteeing fiscal resources and the function of enabling fiscal equalization. The first of these issues is the significance and the level of the guarantee of fiscal resources: the mechanism by which the government obliges local administrations to provide specified public services, and its relationship with cost-cutting measures. The second issue is the definition of fiscal capability and the index employed to determine fiscal capability. The third is the relative positioning of local governments which do not receive allocation tax grants. Disparities between municipalities increase conspicuously with an increase in local fiscal resources. This chapter discusses the introduction of an alternative system of negative allocation tax grants.

Keywords Allocation of intergovernmental functions • Local allocation tax • Guarantee of fiscal resources • Cost-cutting measures • Disparities in fiscal capability • Fiscal demand • Local governments which do not receive allocation tax grants • Negative allocation tax • Separation of functions

---

W. Kobayashi (✉)
Faculty of Policy Informatics, Chiba University of Commerce, Chiba, Japan

T. Hatta (ed.), *Economic Challenges Facing Japan's Regional Areas*,
https://doi.org/10.1007/978-981-10-7110-2_18

1 Introduction

Discussion of fiscal decentralization eventually arrives at the question of the allocation of functions and the allocation of fiscal resources. The former involves the question of what role local public authorities (local governments) should play, and the latter the question of how fiscal resources should be allocated in relation to these roles.

Traditionally, discussion of the allocation of functions between governments has classified the roles of the governments based on the concept of the three functions of public finance, and, in relation to the function of allocation of resources, has considered allocation by local governments as the most efficient means of provision of local public goods ("the decentralization theorem"). However, when we take externality and disparities in fiscal capability between regions into consideration, issues in relation to an absolute reliance on local governments for the provision of local public goods become apparent, suggesting the need for the apportioning of specific roles in intergovernmental fiscal transfers.[1]

In Japan, the local allocation tax and national treasury disbursements are positioned as representative systems for the transfer of public finance between administrations. The former are general grants, the use of which is not specified, while the latter are special grants for specified purposes. The local allocation tax is considered to have two functions, the guarantee of fiscal resources and fiscal equalization; national treasury disbursements also play a role in the function of guaranteeing fiscal resources. Intergovernmental fiscal transfers raise numerous issues; this chapter considers three issues related to the two functions indicated above.

2 The Guarantee of Fiscal Resources: Significance and Level

The first issue to be considered is the significance and level of the guarantee of fiscal resources. In Japan's system of regional finances, part of the expenses entailed by the public services that it is mandatory for a regional public body to provide is supplied by the central government as a treasury disbursement, and the remaining expense for the municipality concerned is calculated as a local allocation tax grant, and provided to individual public bodies in accordance with their financial status. Under this system, then, the financing for some public services is guaranteed by treasury disbursements and local allocation tax grants.

Table 18.1 Traditional theory of the distribution of roles between governments

Resource allocation function		*Income redistribution function*	*Economic stabilization function*
Local public goods	*National public goods*		
Local government	National government	National government	National government

Source: Prepared by author based on Oates (1972)

The significance of the guarantee of fiscal resources must therefore be considered in tandem with the significance of the system under which the central government obliges municipalities to provide specific public services. According to the traditional view of the distribution of functions shown in Table 18.1, in addition to supplying national public goods, the national government should also fulfill an income redistribution function and an economic stabilization function. The question is whether, in fulfilling these functions, it is desirable for the national government to create local agencies in regional areas and assign national public servants to perform the relevant duties, or whether the performance of the functions should be entrusted to local governments and undertaken by local public servants. This is an issue that should be given prudent consideration in every area of administration.[2]

For example, in the case of the social security system, a representative income redistribution measure, the government sets standards and so forth, and these are put into effect by municipalities. The traditional view of the distribution of functions considers the social security system as one that should be administered by the central government, but it is not essential that the central government should be responsible for the implementation of the system. The rationale for the assertion that the central government should be responsible for redistributive measures is the concern that, if redistributive measures were entrusted to municipalities, redistribution would not be appropriately implemented due to a desire to avoid an influx of lower-income residents and an exodus of higher-income residents in municipalities offering a generous redistribution of income. It is considered acceptable for municipalities to implement the social security system if the government fulfills the role of setting standards and guarantees uniform operation of the system.[3]

With regard to the level of the guarantee of fiscal resources, it will be necessary to examine a number of fundamental approaches: Should essential expenses be guaranteed unconditionally; should the government guarantee essential expenses after local governments have undertaken standard measures for the reduction of costs; or should essential expenses be guaranteed after the most extensive cost-cutting measures able to be conceived have been implemented? While an unconditional guarantee of resources raises concerns over potential blowouts in local government expenses, a guarantee of the minimum essential resources produces concerns over shortfalls in fiscal resources, and fiscal disparities between regions generating disparities in terms of citizen welfare. Considered from this perspective, the provision of fiscal resources based on standard cost-cutting measures seems the ideal choice, but the issue here is how to define, and how to measure, essential expenses with standard cost-cutting measures as a precondition.

Ordinary local allocation tax, which represents more than 90% of the total of local allocation tax, is allocated to the figure remaining when standard fiscal revenue is subtracted from standard fiscal demand (i.e., it is equivalent to the shortfall in fiscal resources). The function of the local allocation tax in guaranteeing fiscal resources is actualized by means of this calculation method. As a mechanism to make it possible to project fiscal demand as accurately as possible while preventing increases in expenses, variables which it is difficult for local governments to manipulate at their own discretion (population, area, etc.) are the fundamental units of measurement, and these are multiplied by unit expenses calculated from standard expenses (projected expenditure by local governments providing for standard eventualities) and correction factors taking into consideration the status of individual local governments.

In addition, a "top-runner" system was introduced in FY 2016. Under this system, expenditure by local governments which have controlled their expenses by means of the use of outsourcing or the introduction of the "designated manager system" for certain areas of their duties is reflected in the calculation of total expenses. This can be interpreted as a partial transition from a guarantee of standard fiscal resources to a guarantee of the minimum fiscal resources. However, in evaluating this system, it will be essential to consider how the appropriate level of guaranteed resources is conceptualized, and what degree of financial disparity between regions is allowable.

3 Fiscal Capability: Definition and Indicators

The second issue for consideration is the definition of fiscal capability and the determination of indicators for this parameter. The fiscal equalization function of the local allocation tax primarily equalizes disparities in fiscal capability between localities, and can be interpreted as a means of equalizing disparities in demand and disparities in revenue based on the standard local allocation tax discussed above.[4] The higher the regional revenue, chiefly sourced from local taxes, the lower the allocation tax; the higher the fiscal demand, that is, the higher the essential expenses, the higher the local allocation tax.

From this perspective, it would be natural to assume that fiscal capability can be defined as the level of fiscal revenue in relation to fiscal demand. In fact, in Japan's local government finance system, the three-year average of the figure obtained by dividing the standard fiscal revenue by standard fiscal demand is defined as the fiscal capability index, and is employed as an indicator of the fiscal capability of local governments. However, there are differing opinions as to whether to include fiscal demand in the definition of fiscal capability, or to recognize disparity in demand (disparity in costs) as part of the disparity in fiscal capability which is to be equalized. In attempting to gain an accurate understanding of fiscal demand, a system in which actual expenses or scheduled expenses are allocated separately to each local government may be considered, but the amount received in the allocation would increase by the amount expended for the operation of the system, generating the possibility of an increase in expenses. This issue is similar to the point of contention regarding the level for the guarantee of fiscal resources.

At the same time, even if fiscal capability were to be defined based exclusively on fiscal revenue, the figure would normally be divided by population. Division by population can be considered to provide an objective indicator of the fiscal scale of the local government in question, and it is possible to perceive an awareness of fiscal demand in the background. When defining fiscal capability, it is therefore not possible to ignore fiscal demand, but it is also not absolutely necessary for the indicator which expresses true fiscal capability and the fiscal capability which is the subject of the fiscal equalization system to be the same. Even if the fiscal capability which is the subject of the fiscal equalization system diverges from true fiscal capability, if this is the result of a measure to prevent an increase in expenses, the system can be considered to be rational.

4 Positioning of Local Governments Not Receiving Allocation Tax Grants

The third issue is the positioning of local governments not receiving allocation tax grants. These are local governments which do not receive the normal allocation tax grant because their standard fiscal revenue exceeds their standard fiscal demand. In a situation in which such local governments exist, disparities between regions expand conspicuously with an increase in local sources of tax revenue. Table 18.2 shows a simple numerical example of this phenomenon.

In Table 18.2, we assume the existence of two hypothetical local governments, A and B, the level of standard fiscal demand of each of which is designated as 100. Standard tax revenue is the tax revenue considered to be obtainable by the local government when the tax items specified by the Local Tax Act are levied at the standard taxation rate. Standard fiscal revenue is this amount multiplied by 0.75.[5] When the amount determined by subtracting standard fiscal revenue from standard fiscal demand is positive, the ordinary allocation tax grant is the figure obtained; when the figure is negative, the ordinary allocation tax grant is zero. In the numerical example shown in Table 18.2, A is a local government which does not receive allocation tax grants. CV in the column at the right of the table is the coefficient of variance (standard deviation divided by the average value), which shows the magnitude of variation between the variables in each column (i.e., the magnitude of disparity between the local governments).

Table 18.2 Increase in standard tax revenue and expansion of disparity between municipalities

Local government	*A*	*B*	*Total*	*CV*
Standard fiscal demand	100	100	200	0.000
Standard tax revenue	160	40	200	0.600
Standard fiscal revenue	120	30	150	0.600
Ordinary allocation tax	0	70	70	1.000
Standard tax + Allocation tax	160	110	270	0.185
Standard fiscal demand	100	100	200	0.000
Standard tax revenue	192	48	240	0.600
Standard fiscal revenue	144	36	180	0.600
Ordinary allocation tax	0	64	64	1.000
Standard tax + Allocation tax	192	112	304	0.263

The lower section of Table 18.2 shows a scenario in which the standard taxation revenue of each administration increases by a factor of 1.2 against the upper section of the table. Because tax revenue increases by the same proportion for each municipality, there is no change in the coefficient of variance, but considered from the perspective of general fiscal resources including allocation tax (standard tax + local allocation tax), the coefficient of variance increases by approximately 40% (0.185 → 0.263). This is because in the case of the municipality receiving allocation tax grants, 75% of the increase in tax revenue is cancelled out by a reduction in the amount of the grant, while in the case of the municipality which does not receive an allocation tax grant, the increase remains 100%, and this figure represents revenue for the municipality.

Table 18.3 shows a scenario in which standard fiscal revenue exceeds standard fiscal demand, and the difference (the excess amount of fiscal resources) is recorded as a negative allocation tax amount. In this scenario, the effect of increased tax revenue in increasing the disparity in ordinary fiscal resources is around 15% (0.120 → 0.138). According to the concept of a negative income tax, an individual whose taxable income fell below a minimum threshold would receive the difference as a grant from the government; under a system of negative allocation tax, a municipality recording a negative figure when standard fiscal revenue was subtracted from standard fiscal demand would pay the difference to the government.

Naturally, fierce opposition to the introduction of a negative allocation tax system could be expected from municipalities not receiving allocation tax grants. In order to resolve the issue by other means, it would be

Table 18.3 Negative allocation tax and increase in standard tax revenue

Local government	*A*	*B*	*Total*	*CV*
Standard fiscal demand	100	100	200	0.000
Standard tax revenue	160	40	200	0.600
Standard fiscal revenue	120	30	150	0.600
Ordinary allocation tax	−20	70	50	1.800
Standard tax + Allocation tax	140	110	250	0.120
Standard fiscal demand	100	100	200	0.000
Standard tax revenue	192	48	240	0.600
Standard fiscal revenue	144	36	180	0.600
Ordinary allocation tax	−44	64	20	5.400
Standard tax + Allocation tax	148	112	260	0.138

necessary to make all local governments recipients of allocation tax grants. This would necessitate measures to integrate part of the national treasury disbursement with the local allocation tax and increase the amount of standard fiscal demand, or to transform some local taxes into national taxes, and reduce standard fiscal revenue. The former, however, runs counter to the concept of separation of functions, which holds that the local allocation tax's functions of guaranteeing fiscal resources and equalizing public finances should be kept separate.[6] In the background of the argument for the separation of functions in relation to intergovernmental fiscal transfers lies the sense that the integration of multiple functions in a special system would make the relative positioning of each specific system vague, leading to a lack of accountability. This is consistent with the point made in this chapter that the significance of the guarantee of fiscal resources and the definition of fiscal capability should be re-examined. It will be necessary to give consideration to a number of issues, including the relative positioning of local governments which do not receive allocation tax grants.

The second of the measures mentioned above resembles a recent systemic reform in which part of the corporate inhabitant tax was made a national tax under the name of the local corporation tax, but its purpose differs.[7] In addition to reducing the uneven distribution of local tax by making the (significantly unevenly distributed) corporate inhabitant tax a national tax, the aim of this reform was to correct the expansion of disparities in fiscal capability between local governments not receiving allocation tax grants and local governments receiving allocation tax grants, as shown in Table 18.2, by increasing the local consumption tax rate. This would increase the relative weight of local consumption tax, which is very stable and is comparatively evenly distributed among regions. Nevertheless, the relative positioning of local governments which do not receive allocation tax grants in the fiscal equalization system remains an issue which should be examined prudently in considering the necessary future direction for Japan's local taxation system.

Notes

1. This discussion of the allocation of functions between governments based on the three functions of public finance and expected roles in intergovernmental fiscal transfers is based on Oates (1972).
2. The issue of spillover of local public goods is also an important point for discussion. This refers to the problem of the benefit of local public goods provided to a specific region spreading to another region. The fact that a

local government is an entity which has an interest in and responsibility for the welfare of the residents of its region, and does not consider external benefit extending to other regions, may result in the provision of an insufficient level of public goods by the local government. One method of responding to this issue is to provide incentives via percentage grants. However, because the level of external benefit differs for each project or service, calculation of the appropriate grant rate is difficult. There remains room for discussion as to whether an average grant rate should be set and the remainder left up to the judgment of the relevant municipality, or whether the national government should formulate a basic plan and assume a leadership role.

3. For the distribution of functions between administrative entities in Japan's social security system, see Abe et al. (2008).
4. The fiscal equalization function of the local allocation tax system can also be considered in terms of vertical fiscal equalization, which equalizes the fiscal gap between the national government and local governments, and horizontal fiscal equalization, which equalizes the disparities in fiscal capability between local governments.
5. Some standard tax revenue is also factored into standard fiscal revenue on a 100% basis. The calculation of standard fiscal revenue based on standard tax revenue means that taxes levied independently by the municipality (when it establishes taxes other than legally specified taxes or applies excess taxation at a higher rate than the standard taxation rate) are not reflected in the calculation of the normal allocation tax. In other words, the system is designed to ensure that the local allocation tax does not decline even if the municipality levies its own taxes, which would reduce the incentive for the levying of independent taxes.
6. For the concept of the separation of functions of the local allocation tax, see Sato (2011).
7. The local corporation tax has been applied since the business year commencing in October 2014.

References

Abe, Aya, Kunieda, Shigeki, Suzuki, Wataru, & Hayashi, Masayoshi (2008), *Seikatsuhogo no Keizaibunseki* (Social Welfare: An Economic Analysis), University of Tokyo Press (in Japanese).

Oates, Wallace E. (1972), *Fiscal Federalism*, Harcourt Brace Jovanovich, Inc.

Sato, Motohiro (2011), *Chihozei kaikaku no keizaigaku* (Economics of Local Tax Reform), Nikkei Publishing Inc (in Japanese).

CHAPTER 19

Decentralization Reform and Property Tax in Japan: A Consideration of the Benefit Principle

Tomomi Miyazaki

Abstract This chapter reviews the relationship between property tax and the benefit principle in Japan. Based on Miyazaki and Sato (2011), the author first demonstrates that property tax is not a benefit tax for the supply side because the conditions for tax capitalization, one of the foundations of the "benefit view" with regard to property tax, cannot be satisfied under Japan's current local taxation system. This should be attributed to three factors: limitation of the authority of municipalities to set tax rates, certain preferential property tax programs for land, and the possibility that property tax is a capital tax in effect. The author proposes granting municipalities complete discretion in deciding tax rates and repealing preferential tax programs to make property tax function as a benefit tax.

Keywords Property tax in Japan • Benefit principle • Tax capitalization • Preferential property tax programs • Benefit view • Capital tax view • Greater local government autonomy • Abolition of tax on houses

T. Miyazaki (✉)
Graduate School of Economics, Kobe University, Hyogo, Japan

T. Hatta (ed.), *Economic Challenges Facing Japan's Regional Areas*,
https://doi.org/10.1007/978-981-10-7110-2_19

1 The Benefit Principle of Property Tax

Some researchers have proposed that after the decentralization reform in Japan, property tax can be useful as a fundamental tax for municipalities. For example, Ihori (2007) argues that a property tax could be employed as an effective tax under the decentralized society because it enables the benefit of local government public services to be reflected in a tax.

This argument presupposes that a property tax satisfies the benefit principle. According to the traditional view of the incidence of property tax, the burden of a property tax on land is borne fully by the owner of the land. If this is the case, a property tax on land can be considered to satisfy the benefit principle. On the basis of this argument, Doi (2000) proposes that a property tax on land should be a fundamental tax for municipalities.

However, in reality, a property tax is levied not only on land but also on houses and depreciable assets. This chapter provides an introduction to previous research concerning the relationship between decentralization and property tax and considers the problems of the current property tax system, and concludes by offering a suggestion as to the best direction for the property tax system after the decentralization reform.

The benefit principle of property tax is explained by the benefit view on tax incidence. The benefit view states that while property tax increases the tax burden, this burden is offset by the benefits offered by public services financed by the tax. This proposition is explained using the example of rental properties. Let us assume that a property tax is levied on rental houses, and the tax revenue is used for the construction of a shopping mall operated by the local government. The construction of the shopping mall can be considered to make the local area more attractive, and thus to increase the asset value of residential properties. This is called "tax capitalization." This capitalization offsets the decline in the landlord's profit due to the levying of the tax. For the renter of the property, even if the rental fee increases as a result of the tax, the convenience thanks to the shopping mall will be considered to be worth an increase of this amount, or in some cases even more. The benefit view explains the offsetting of tax burden by the benefits received from public services in this way.

In research conducted in the USA, Carroll and Yinger (1994) examined the benefit view via an analysis of 147 towns and districts in the Boston metropolitan area. They concluded that the owners of rental prop-

Table 19.1 Results of numerical calculations for current system (Miyazaki and Sato 2011)

	Case of public investment	*Case of local government expenditure*
Net burden on property owners	−7.587	−5.675
Net burden on renters	0.00621	0.00166

Source: All figures are derived from Miyazaki and Sato (2011) sample mean values

erties bear some tax burden in the form of a decline in their profit rate following the levying of the tax, and that as a result, the benefit view does not hold in the strict sense.

In Japan, Miyazaki and Sato (2011) studied the benefit view by means of an econometric analysis and simple calculations using data for 46 prefectures. Table 19.1 shows the results of the numerical calculations conducted in this research. The net tax burden on renters was 0.00621% in the case in which public investment is considered a municipal public service, and 0.00166% in the case in which local government expenditure is considered a public service. Both results are close to zero, suggesting that for renters, the benefit provided by public services adequately offsets the burden of the tax. By contrast, the figures for the net benefit received by property owners are both negative, indicating only a decline in the profit rate for property owners. This result indicates that because the capitalization touched on above is inadequate, under the present system the property tax is not a benefit tax for property owners.

2 Problems of the Existing Property Tax System

The following three factors can be considered as reasons why the current property tax system is not a benefit tax.

First, local governments have not been granted complete authority in setting tax rates. The benefit view assumes that a municipality selects a tax rate that enables the benefit to counterbalance the burden of the tax. In the case of Japan, the standard rate for property tax is set at 1.4%, and while municipalities have the right to impose, for example, an exceeded tax rate, there is virtually no discretion for them to freely determine their own rate of property tax.

The second factor is whether or not the benefit from public services is appropriately reflected in market prices (land prices). When there is a gap between tax bases and market price, the capitalization mechanism does not function. The discussion of problems related to methods of assessment for land in the property tax bases relies chiefly on Sato (2011).

Land is revalued every three years; since 1994, the yardstick for the assessed value of land has been 70% of the declared land value. While the system attempts to a certain extent to reflect market prices, it also features a variety of preferential measures. For example, in the case of a small residence, the tax base is one-sixth of the assessed value. Taking these preferential measures into consideration, Nakano (2004) points out that the effective tax rate on land is low, in actuality only 0.098%. In the case of a normal housing lot with an area of over 200 square meters, the tax base is one-third of the assessed value. Preferential measures such as these reduce the burden of the property tax when land is owned for residence. The land zoned for business purposes can be between 60 and 70% of the assessed value.[1]

Turning to agricultural land, in the case of agricultural land located in urbanization control zones, which is in principle not to be used for development purposes or for the construction of city facilities, assessed values and tax bases are, in principle, equivalent to those for residential land, in particular within Japan's three major metropolitan areas. However, in the case of normal agricultural land and agricultural land located in urbanization control zones other than those mentioned above, mechanisms including measures to ease the tax burden in response to the classification of the level of burden ensure that tax bases are discounted.[2] As can be seen from the discussion above, as a result of various preferential measures, under the existing system tax bases are discounted.

The third reason is the possibility that property tax might be considered a capital tax following a local public finance theory. Carroll and Yinger (1994) and Miyazaki and Sato (2011) indicate that the burden of the property tax extends to the supply side. Let me consider the levying of taxes on capital, in particular on residential buildings and other depreciable assets, based on the capital tax view. Assume a country made up of two regions: region A, in which the tax rate is higher than the national average, and region B, in which the tax rate is lower than the national average. First, the rate of return on investment for capital temporarily declines in both regions due to taxation, and there is a flow of capital from region A to region B as a result of the tax rate gap (an excise tax effect). Next, due to oversupply in region B as a result of the capital inflow, the post-tax rate of return on capital in region B declines further, to a level lower than that resulting from the excise tax effect (this is a profit tax effect). If capital tax view is assumed to be correct, then a property tax can be interpreted as a capital tax rather than a benefit tax. Miyazaki and Sato (2013) examined the capital tax view with a focus on residential buildings, and found that the property tax is incident on the owners of capital. The empirical results produced by Miyazaki and Sato (2013) suggest that the current property tax may have an aspect as a capital tax.

3 Property Tax under Conditions of Greater Local Government Autonomy

Section 19.2 indicated the possibility that Japan's current property tax is not a benefit tax based on three factors: (1) Municipal governments possess only limited rights to determine the taxation rate; (2) There is a gap between tax bases and market prices as a result of various preferential measures; and (3) The inclusion of capital as an object of the tax makes it, for practical purposes, a capital tax. In this section I will make some suggestions for property tax after the decentralization reform.

First, after the decentralization reform, it would be necessary to grant municipalities complete discretion in deciding tax rates. Miyazaki and Sato (2011) also conducted numerical calculations for a case in which municipalities possess complete discretion in setting tax rates under a decentralized society. In this case, property tax revenues and the provision of public services are directly linked. The results are shown in Fig. 19.1. The net burden on property owners is close to zero in most regions, as a result of the offsetting of the decline in the profit rate due to the property tax by the benefit received from public services.

However, if the various preferential measures causing taxation standards to diverge from market prices and the differences in assessment methods for land being used for different purposes were to remain in place, even if local governments were granted the right to set tax rates, the benefit received from pubic services would not be adequately reflected in land prices. Because of this, the property tax would not function exclusively as a benefit tax even in the decentralized society. In order for the property tax to function as a benefit tax, it would be necessary to grant municipalities the right to set property tax rates, while at the same time

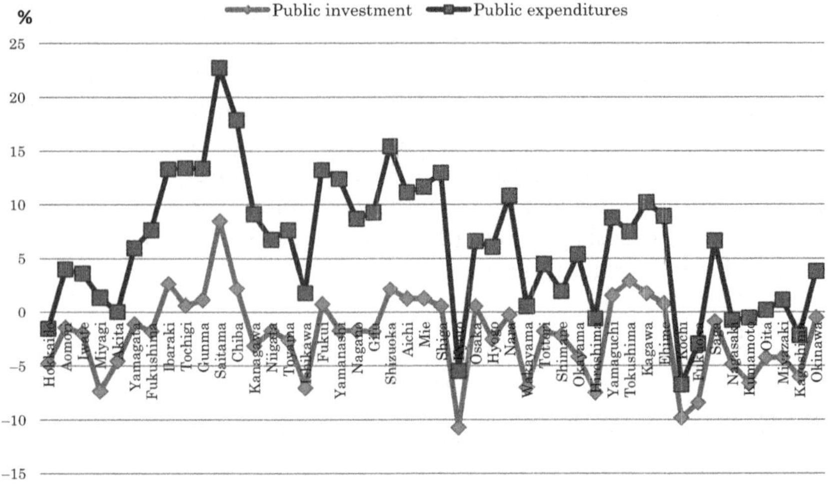

Fig. 19.1 Results of measurement of net burden on property owners. Note: "Public investment" shows the case in which municipal public services are considered to be a public investment, and "Public expenditures" shows the case in which municipal public services are considered to be a municipal expenditure. Source: Miyazaki and Sato (2011, p. 115)

eliminating preferential measures from the tax bases. Sato (2011) points out that it would be desirable for the measures to be reflected in the tax rate so that preferential measures are in effect. This goal would be realized if municipalities were granted complete discretion in setting tax rates under the decentralized society.

In order to make it possible to realize the operation of local government finances situated in a direct relationship with residents, it would be necessary to awaken an awareness of costs in those residents and spur an interest in the management of local finances, by granting local governments complete freedom in setting the tax rate and eliminating preferential measures from the taxation standards, rendering the link between property tax and public services transparent.

Turning to other objects of taxation, in the case of depreciable assets, as suggested by Sato (2011), it would be necessary to avoid incentives for tax competition or tax exporting. It would also be necessary to reform the property tax on residential buildings, which, as Miyazaki and Sato (2013) showed, functions as a capital tax. As discussed above, Miyazaki and Sato (2011) consider that a tax on residences, including rental houses, could satisfy the benefit principle after the decentralized reform. However, taking the effect of the distribution of resources into consideration, the abolition of a tax on residential buildings, achieving revenue neutrality by increasing the burden of tax on land, as proposed by Yamazaki (2011), also represents another option.

Notes

1. See Research Center for Property Assessment System (ed.) (2015), etc.
2. http://www.maff.go.jp/j/keiei/koukai/nouchi_seido/pdf/hoyuu_zeisei.pdf (in Japanese).

References

Carroll, R. J., & Yinger J. (1994), "Is the Property Tax a Benefit Tax? The Case of Rental Housing," *National Tax Journal* 47 (2), pp. 295–316.

Doi, Takero (2000), "*Chihokofuzei no mondai to sono kaikaku* (Issues and Reforms of Local Allocation Tax)," *Ekonomikkusu: Economics & Policy*, 3, pp. 70–79, Toyo Keizai Inc (in Japanese).

Ihori, Toshihiro (2007), '*Chiisana seifu' no otoshiana: itami naki zaiseisaiken rosen wa kiken da* (Traps of 'Small Government': Danger in Policies of Fiscal Reform without Pain), Nikkei Publishing Inc (in Japanese).

Miyazaki, Tomomi, & Sato, Motohiro (2011), "Is Property Tax a Benefit Tax? The Case of Japanese Regions," *Economic Analysis*, No.184, pp. 99–119 (in Japanese).

Miyazaki, Tomomi, & Sato, Motohiro (2013), "Is the Property Tax a Capital Tax? An Investigation of the 'Capital Tax View' of the Property Tax," *The Economic Review*, Vol. 65, No. 4, pp. 303–317 (in Japanese).

Nakano, Hideo (2004), "*Koteishisanzei kaikaku to tochi/juutaku shijo* (Property Tax Reform and Land & Housing Market)," Finance, June 2004, pp. 64–70 (in Japanese).

Research Center for Property Assessment System (ed.) (2015), *Koteshisanzei no Shiori* (Guidebook for Property Tax) (in Japanese).

Sato, Motohiro (2011), *Chihozei kaikaku no keizaigaku* (Economics of Local Tax Reform), Nikkei Publishing Inc (in Japanese).

Yamazaki, Fukuju (2011), "*Shijo-mekanizumu wo tsujita hisaichi no kon-nan to fukko kosuto no kyoyu* (Sharing difficulty and recovery costs at disaster affected areas using a market mechanism)," in S. Ito, M. Okuno, T. Onishi and M. Hanazaki (eds.), *Higashinihon daisinnsai fukkou heno teigen: jizoku kanou na keizaishakai no kouchiku* (Proposals for recovery from the Great East Japan Earthquake: Building a sustainable economy/society), University of Tokyo Press, pp. 264–270 (in Japanese).

Index[1]

[1] Note: Page numbers followed by 'n' refer to note.

T. Hatta (ed.), *Economic Challenges Facing Japan's Regional Areas*,
https://doi.org/10.1007/978-981-10-7110-2

The manufacturer's authorised representative in the EU is Springer Nature Customer Service Centre GmbH, Europaplatz 3, 69115 Heidelberg, Germany. If you have any concerns regarding our products, please contact ProductSafety@springernature.com

Printed and bound by CPI Group (UK) Ltd, Croydon, CR0 4YY
30/09/2026
02225451-0003